The
END *of* INFLUENCE

*What Happens When Other
Countries Have the Money*

STEPHEN S. COHEN
J. BRADFORD DeLONG

BASIC BOOKS
A MEMBER OF THE PERSEUS BOOKS GROUP
New York

Books published by Basic Books are available at special discounts for
bulk purchases in the United States by corporations, institutions, and
other organizations. For more information, please contact the Special
Markets Department at the Perseus Books Group, 2300 Chestnut
Street, Suite 200, Philadelphia, PA 19103, or call (800) 810-4145, ext.
5000, or e-mail special.markets@perseusbooks.com.

Designed by Timm Bryson

The Library of Congress has cataloged the hardcover as follows:
Cohen, Stephen S.
   The end of influence : what happens when other countries have the
money / Stephen S. Cohen, J. Bradford DeLong.
      p. cm.
Includes index.
   ISBN 978-0-465-01876-5 (alk. paper)
   1. International economic relations—21st century. 2. Power (Social
sciences)—United States. 3. Debts, External—United States. 4.
United States—Foreign economic relations. I. De Long, J. Bradford.
II. Title.
   HF1359.C6527 2010
   337—dc22

                                                                2009031206

Paperback ISBN: 978-0-465-02454-4
e-book ISBN: 978-0-465-02007-2

10 9 8 7 6 5 4 3 2 1

PRAISE FOR
THE END OF INFLUENCE

"Stephen S. Cohen and J. Bradford DeLong vividly describe the evaporation of American economic power and what it is likely to mean for the United States and the world."
—Forbes.com

"In this reasoned chronicle of worldwide fiscal and cultural influence from pre–WWI to the present, Berkeley academics Cohen and DeLong measure the rise and decline of US prestige, concluding that the era of US dominance is over. . . . Cohen and DeLong craft a chilling portrait of the country's accelerating fiscal woes."
—*Publishers Weekly*

"Stephen S. Cohen and J. Bradford DeLong find a worldwide reaction against what are perceived to be the excesses and defects of neo-liberalism. . . . Suggested study."
—*Business Line*

"Lucid explanations are offered of trade deficits, currency fluctuations, and the like, and the cause of the current crisis located in the ballooning of finance as a proportion of the US economy."
—*The Guardian*

"Cohen and DeLong's interesting look at the real New World Order is worthy of consideration as it describes a reality that's fast approaching."
—*Miami Herald*

"DeLong and Cohen . . . contribute to our knowledge of how the world actually works."
—*The National Interest*

"The implications of the current financial crisis go beyond its multiplier effect of impoverishing the global economy. Many experts and economists have been predicting the end of America's economic hegemony and Stephen Cohen and Bradford DeLong illustrate this imminent scenario."
—*Business World*

"One of the central virtues of the book is the sustained attention Cohen and DeLong give to some of the lazy assumptions we make about the American economy."
—*National Review Online*

FOR
Eleanor

AND FOR
Michael and Gianna

CONTENTS

ACKNOWLEDGMENTS

Research for this book received generous support from the Alfred P. Sloan Foundation and from the European Union Center of Excellence, UC Berkeley, and benefited from the excellent research assistance of Estafania Santacreu-Vasut.

ONE

Introduction: When Other Countries Have the Money

During World War I, the world's long-reigning superpower, Great Britain, faced a disturbing development: Just when the nation really needed it, Britain no longer had the money. The money had shifted to the United States, where it accumulated for the next sixty years, and then began to drain away. Soon it will be gone.

The money is not likely to come back anytime soon. The United States is now the world's biggest debtor, and there is no other debtor nation of consequence. The legendary Spanish bullfighter Garcia was once asked: "Who is the world's greatest matador?" His prompt reply: "Me, Garcia the Great. And there is no number two, and no number three."

Does it matter? Yes. Back when the United States had the money, it mattered for Americans and it mattered more for others. The American government could and did use its public money and could and did channel the private money of

Americans in what it regarded as its own, the nation's, and the world's interest. Having the money was a powerful tool and force. America, of course, used its economic dominance exclusively for global good. The United States gave market forces free play—except when it needed to apply financial pressure to encourage other countries to do right—to do what was good for the world and themselves, and to eschew doing wrong. With the Marshall Plan, the United States strongly encouraged European politicians to adopt the mixed-economy, social-democratic order of the post–World War II North Atlantic.* With hints that it would not support the pound or the franc, America forced Britain and France to abandon their ill-conceived colonial adventure in Suez. In these ways and others, America, of course, used the leverage of having the money exclusively for global good—but it was the American government that decided what was globally good.

When you have the money—and "you" are a big, economically and culturally vital nation—you get more than just a higher standard of living for your citizens. You get power and influence, and a much-enhanced ability to act out. When the money drains out, you can maintain the edge in living standards of your citizens for a considerable time (as long as others are willing to hold your growing debt and pile interest payments on top). But you lose power, especially the power to ignore others, quite quickly—though hopefully, in quiet, nonconfrontational ways. And you lose influence—the ability to have

---

* Notes and references to this book are to be found online at www.cohen-delong-influence.com.

your wishes, ideas, and folkways willingly accepted, eagerly copied, and absorbed into daily life by others. As with good parenting, you hope that by the time this happens, those ideas and ways have been so thoroughly integrated that they have become part of what is normal and regular abroad as well as at home; sometimes, of course, they don't. In either case, the end is inevitable: you must become, recognize that you have become, and act like a normal country. For America, this will be a shock: America has not been a normal country for a long, long time.

HOW WILL IT MATTER?

If international financial transactions were exclusively market exchanges between private players focused just on the highest profits, it wouldn't matter much who had the money or where those with the money happened to live. But often it does matter. In times of emergencies, the private property of a country's citizens and of its national-flag companies is always controlled by its political master, government. And private market transactions are not the whole game; they never were. Sometimes, significant portions of the money are directly controlled by nonmarket, political actors. Today is one of those times. Lots of the money is now in the hands of the governments of oil-producing states—ranging from Norway to Russia and the countries of the Persian Gulf. And much is in the hands of the governments of Asian manufacturing countries. Perhaps these nonmarket actors will act like normal market players, maximizing secure returns.

The "great and the good" of the North Atlantic (and some from honorary North Atlantic nations) in their various forums and institutions are trying to get sovereign wealth funds and other government-managed and government-influenced asset pools to act like the giant pension funds of California civil servants or like the exemplary sovereign wealth fund of omni-exemplary, oil-rich Norway investing prudently for long-term returns, confining their non-bottom-line behavior to proudly shunning a few tainted categories of companies such as tobacco or armaments, and transparently posting their investments for scrutiny.

The great and the good seek codes of behavior that aim to oblige sovereign wealth funds—in a nonbinding way—to pretend that they are market actors seeking only secure investment returns, to be transparent, and not to operate at more than the margins as agents of political strategy or of zero-global-sum national industrial policy. A country that accepts sovereign wealth funds' investments into its territory could then pretend that it does not have to care about the identity or purposes of the foreign politicians who have deployed their nations' wealth. The problems and complexities then go away, or are at least reduced to manageable proportions, and the great and the good will help to manage them.

A second possibility is that with time and good behavior— calm, wise leadership and dialogue—the puzzle posed by giant investment funds controlled by governments will no longer be threatening; it will shrink from a six-hundred-pound tiger to a mere house cat. Like all government-controlled surpluses, sovereign wealth funds and their like could be quickly drained into domestic maws, either by populist excess (à la Chavez in Venezuela) or by responses to sudden economic difficulties, and used to sustain domestic employment and companies. When oil prices fell off their recent peak, Russia's huge sovereign wealth fund suddenly disgorged hundreds of billions to support Russian banks and companies and, as an unintended outcome, calmed nerves outside Russia. In this way, the sovereign wealth funds of oil producers could defang themselves and become something much closer to the rainy-day funds they were initially intended to be, where safety and liquidity become the prime considerations in the placement of the money. And over time, the "excess savings" that engorge government funds in China and the other Asian manufacturers can slowly be shifted from accumulating foreign assets into much-needed domestic consumption.

Finally, the great and the good are quite right in what they whisper: If you owe the bank $1 million, the bank has you; if you owe $1 billion, you have the bank. The implication is that China, the biggest and most important holder of U.S. debt, is trapped into a strange, unwanted, and uncomfortable embrace with the indebted United States. The Chinese government holds about $2.5 trillion in foreign reserves, probably 70 percent of that in U.S. obligations. This comes to over $20,000 per U.S. household; there is no way the United States could readily pay it back. Because it also amounts to about half of China's GDP, China can't just write it off.

Thus, China and the United States are economically codependent, the producer and the consumer, the creditor and the debtor. One nation spends more than it produces and has to borrow to buy, and the other nation produces more than it spends and has to lend the difference to buyers to keep production going. We're bound together, and we must manage this mutual dependence carefully and, over time, wind down those economic imbalances. Populist reactions in the United States and in China must be avoided. The United States and China must also begin to work more broadly as partners to stabilize a world in political, social, and economic disarray.

So perhaps it won't matter, at least not very much. We can hope. But one thing is sure: Absent an international economic catastrophe or a major war or another game-changing disaster, the money will not soon be coming back to America.

THE NEOLIBERAL ORDER AT BAY

The growth of the world economy outside the United States and the accumulation of trade deficits that have made America the world's supreme debtor nation will matter. It will matter still more because if the current financial and economic hurricane does nothing else, it will have demolished the hold of free-market theory that neoliberals have established over the past thirty years as the dominant guide and constraint on government policies: Free up markets; deregulate; privatize; get government out of the economy. Pressed by economic crisis, governments all over the world are taking control of financial and industrial firms, setting out new regulations, and intervening to affect market outcomes. They are tempted and pressured to rescue their big, bleeding firms and their citizens' jobs—a policy called "lemon socialism"—and to deploy their rusted instruments of economic intervention to protect and even enhance the chances of their national firms and workers. And, of course, the governments are pressured to leverage their wealth strategically, rather than invest passively, as simple, though big, market players. All these changes will matter substantially for the United States in at least three important ways.

First, there will be a loss of American power to undertake unilateral foreign-policy actions, to act or to act out as the hyperpower. It is not clear whether this is best viewed as a problem or as an opportunity. The United States now needs to be very wary of actions that could threaten the inflow and stock of foreign private and government-owned capital—just as Britain and France needed to be wary when America had the money. We can't just irk China or the Gulf money pots with impunity. This does not mean that America is dependent on, say, the money managers of China and their political bosses, but it does mean that we are no longer independent of China, either. U.S. financial markets are just too vulnerable to an act of displeasure by China—or even a hint of such an action. An American president is now vulnerable to a sudden crash in the financial markets; he or she is not captured and bound, but is now constrained to think twice and perhaps once again before speaking or acting. That is new. The once-unconstrained giant will now feel the tug of thin cords of gold.

Second, there will be a loss of American soft, or cultural, power. Those who must beseech others for the money always look less worth emulating than those from whom money is besought. To the extent that one views America's democratic, commercial, individualist, consumerist, and cosmopolitan culture as something worth emulating by other countries, then the fact that other countries now have the money is a significant loss.

Third, a serious international return to ambitious pursuit by nation-states of zero-global-sum industrial policies is likely to weaken America's economic position. The United States excels at entrepreneurial and technological invention and innovation, especially at start-ups like Intel, Apple, and Google. What happens when Japan, Germany, or China creates a protected domestic launch market (as John Stuart Mill recommended countries do 161 years ago, 41 years after Alexander Hamilton propounded the same idea), pumps billions into launching photovoltaic or wind-power companies to drive successive rounds of innovation and economies of scale, all in order to take an overpowering lead in a surging new industry in which American firms, dependent on the tight constraints of capital markets, will be left far behind? What happens when the financing for the next generation of American biotech or nanotech start-ups comes from one of Singapore's or China's sovereign wealth funds? What happens when the condition of financing is a demand—legitimately and understandably— that part of the deal be the rapid back-transfer of the new technology? That could matter a lot.

If we are fortunate, we will see U.S. economic growth of about 3 percent per year in real terms over the next two decades. Of this growth, about one-quarter—0.75 percent per year, say—will come from the labor side: more hands with more skills and more education. Another one-quarter will come from the capital side: plant and equipment purchases funded by investors. These two components have a narrow economic logic supporting them: Hands go to work and bring skills and educational capabilities with them because they are paid wages and salaries, and investors bring their funds in anticipation of interest coupons, dividends, and capital gains.

However, fully half of economic growth—1.5 percent per year—comes from technological and organizational progress: innovation. Economic growth arising from innovation is not captured by those who first undertake the innovations, create the technologies, or pioneer the organizations. These important fruits of innovation do not remain confined to the innovators but instead spill out in a capillary fashion into the broader economy, first to those nearby and later to those further away— if there is a later. Ford did not capture the lion's share of the gains from the Ford-invented and Ford-pioneered assembly line—General Motors, Caterpillar, Westinghouse, and many others shared them. Xerox did not capture any of the gains from the invention of the windows-icons-mouse-pointer computer interface—Apple and Microsoft did. Fully half of economic growth is an unrecompensed by-product of what businesses do. It spills out into the local industrial ecosystem. This is an opportunity that governments always have and inevitably will try to seize. In this area—capturing and repatriating the spillover growth of innovation—governments have sought, with some successes and many failures, to make industrial policy. But it is not the only one. There is also protecting and supporting your lemons—steel, autos, farms—and, by easily foreseeable extension, squeezing those same lemons in other countries.

The neoliberal order sought a mutual and balanced reduction of government interventist forces. Technological and organizational progress would still be of immense value and still be realized through largely unintended spillovers from economic decisions taken for other motives. But if the logic of the market ruled, the game would at least be a fair one—in a culturally comfortable, but restricted sense of fair: minimizing direct political influence on national economic outcomes. But the neoliberal policy order is unlikely to survive this downturn intact. Governments that have been practicing industrial policy will up their efforts; several others that had recently sworn off efforts will undoubtedly try again.

Foreign governments may or may not succeed. They will, probably, largely fail. Technology transfer is very hard; the global economy is littered with the bones of unfit "national champion" firms and unsuccessful government-led programs to force, via hothouse measures, the growth of commercially successful, technologically sophisticated, high-wage firms. It is, however, incontestably true that there have also been successes. And not all of them have been in East Asia. France in 1945 was supposed to be a country of small-scale family enterprises and meddling bureaucrats incapable of rapid industrialization or productivity growth. Yet a generation of massive government intervention in the economy, including ownership of a huge swath of big companies in most large-scale industries, from banking to autos, transformed the nation into the economic better of Britain and the equal of Germany.

Even the United States, under the politically protective aegis of defense, spun off fully fledged, advanced industries such as commercial jets and computers—industries that quickly soared to global dominance. What part of U.S. leadership in the advanced sectors would exist in its current form without the Defense Advanced Research Projects Agency (DARPA), the National Institutes of Health (NIH), and U.S. research universities? Jet aircraft in Seattle and biotech and electronics around Boston and California's Silicon Valley were always inconceivable without the Massachusetts Institute of Technology, without Stanford, without NIH, and without the Pentagon.

With the weakening of the neoliberal order, it is overwhelmingly likely that many countries will try state-led development through industrial policy. And these attempts may wreak some damage on the American economy.

The neoliberals were quite right to try to rein in "industrial policy" in many of its various forms: Subsidies, undervaluation of currencies, and outright protection are at best zero-sum from a global point of view. Whenever market outcomes in industry after industry are significantly shaped by the policies of nations supporting their champions, it creates a severe system problem. The market then tilts toward a system of competitive, predatory competition between governments seeking to protect and subsidize profits and jobs at home. Overcapacity and inefficiency grow—unless, of course, some very big nations let their companies and workers be squeezed in the interest of pursuing other goals, like rallying the global West in a Cold War.

THE FUTURE OF THE SYSTEM

For over a generation, at increasing volumes, the United States has absorbed the products of other countries' growth and export policies. From our lofty economic preeminence and our role as leader and keeper of the political as well as economic order, it was our responsibility and seemed to be something we could afford. Japan, for example, protected its home market and promoted its steel, shipbuilding, industrial machinery, and automobile makers, and the United States absorbed Japan's output at the expense of those industries at home. Then China, following suit, structured its breathtaking economic growth on promoting industrial exports. To best achieve this, like the earlier Asian exporters, China held down its exchange rate, domestic prices, and consumption; captured and sterilized the dollar earnings from those exports; and piled them up and lent them back to the United States, where they eventually financed more U.S. purchases of Chinese goods.

China got rather a lot more than just a huge pile of dollars that might lose value; it got fast economic growth at home. The United States got something, too. It was able to spend more than it produced, because other countries were content to hold U.S. dollars. The fact that the United States had the money gave it an exorbitant privilege: Its money power freed America from the external constraints that normal countries encountered when they tried to spend more than they produced. And, of course, it gave America the opportunity, while absorbing more and more routine manufacturing from Asia at the expense of those same industries at home, to shift its own economy into what should have been the "sectors of the future": Over the past ten years, the United States has, to a remarkable extent, shifted its economy into finance. Manufacturing declined significantly as a proportion of what the United States produces (though not so much as a proportion of what

Americans consume), and finance as an industry grew to offset that loss, sustaining the level of output and employment.

Effectively and half-consciously, America restructured its economy. But if finance was the industry of the future, it no longer seems to be a future that many want. The freedom of action that the United States enjoyed because it had the money was squandered.

America must restructure its economy again, and so must the world. Countries that seek to grow cannot all just continue by promoting export-led growth alone. And a United States that no longer has the money or the unshakable credibility of vast economic strength cannot for much longer be the importer of last resort to support the international system of open trade and open financial markets.

The open-markets system relied not just on the much-celebrated invisible hand, but also on a system guarantor. One big economy had to be willing and able to run trade deficits to absorb the others' net exports and to issue debt for others that seek safe assets to hold. The United States has been playing that role to some degree since the start of World War I and, to an ever-growing extent, since the end of World War II. But this role required an America that had the money. What would replace that system is, for most economists and policy makers, a question that cannot even be raised; for the few others, it is as disheartening as it is perplexing.

The broad outlines of what is needed to bring the international system closer to balance without radical, system-level change are clear and generally well understood. Americans must produce more, save more, and spend less. China and other export surplus nations must rely less on exports, consume more, and therefore accumulate less savings that pile up in dollars. The shift must be rather large, and it needs to come slowly—definitely not abruptly—but still somehow convincingly.

Facing up to these limits will be difficult, especially for the United States. American money power has been doubted and weakened. As a result, America will find itself more and more constrained in what it can do and say, politically as well as economically. A United States that no longer has the money will become more and more something of a normal country and less and less the unique hyperpower. The United States will continue to be a world leader—perhaps even *the* leader. But it will no longer be the boss.

The other countries, after all, will have the money.

The Neoliberal Dream Ends

Shrinking Back the State

For over a quarter century now the countries of the world have been dreaming the neoliberals' dream. They have been trying to shrink their states back to their core competencies for two major reasons: (1) promoting economic efficiency, global economic integration, and growth, and (2) avoiding or reducing excess red tape, rent-seeking, and simple corruption. They have been actively privatizing state holdings. They have hugely reduced their ownership and their active involvement in "national champion" companies. They have cut back on interventions to affect market outcomes and on regulation to scrutinize and control market players.

But now they are waking up. And the neoliberals' dream is at an end.

The past decade and a half has seen the sleeper restless, as performance has fallen short of promise. Why has the process of transition in Eastern Europe been accompanied by such a huge rise in inequality and been so suddenly imperiled? How can Argentina be the hero of sober appropriate-government market-oriented development one year and the goat of excessive populist budget deficits four years later? Why did world capital markets send the extremely successful East Asian economies into a terrifying tailspin in 1997–1998? And how has a policy of reliance on private self-regulation spurred by compensation-based incentives landed us with a global financial system in collapse?

This last disquieting question is likely to be decisive. From his seat as chair of the U.S. Federal Reserve, Alan Greenspan presided over much of the quarter century of the neoliberals dream. On October 23, 2008, the chairman reacted to the end of the dream: "Those of us who have looked to the self interest of lending institutions to protect shareholders' equity, myself included, are in a state of shocked disbelief." In the *New York Times,* Edmund Andrews quotes Alan Greenspan's testimony to the House Committee on Oversight and Government Reform. "Do you feel that your ideology pushed you to make decisions that you wish you had not made?" Chairman Henry Waxman asked. "Yes," Greenspan responded.

> I've found a flaw [in my thinking]. I don't know how significant or permanent it is. But I've been very distressed by that fact. . . . This modern risk-management paradigm held sway for decades. The whole intellectual edifice, however, collapsed in the summer of last year.

When the debris from the current crisis is cleared away, it will end with governments having—again—amassed substantial direct and indirect positions in a host of national firms in finance and industry, and having abandoned the presumption that business is not their business. They will find themselves intervening in their economies—through new ownership stakes, nonmarket financing, protection, subsidization, and regulation—in ways and to degrees the neoliberals had, they thought, ended.

Governments will then face an irresistible temptation and considerable political pressure to use their leverage over business for what various groups will regard as the national interest. And when one country does so, it will increase pressure on the others. When the United States bails out its auto industry, or its banks, or insurers, or airlines—shouldn't France and Germany do so, too? If auto plants are going to close in Europe, it matters a lot to Belgian and German politicians whether the closed factories are in Belgium, Germany, or Spain. The position that detailed interventions in industrial location and structure will be disfavored and minimized may be sustainable politically as part of a grand international free-trade bargain among governments, a mutual and balanced reduction in industrial policy deterrence, but deterrence lasts only as long as it actually deters: Once one country has broken the bargain, the rest will be likely to do so as well.

MONEY, POWER, AND INFLUENCE

The coming of World War II ensured that whatever money still remained in Britain left quickly. Franklin Delano Roosevelt ruled an isolationist country that he wished to cajole into engaging in the war with Hitler as early and as completely as he could. But part of Roosevelt's strategy (and a not-altogether-unwelcome consequence, for many who worked in the State, War, and Navy Building—a Victorian-era structure just west of the White House that looked like a French brothel) was to make Britain broke before American taxpayers' money was committed in any way to the fight against Hitler. Only after Britain had sold off the family silver to pay for the nozzle would America "lend" Britain its garden hose to fight the Hitlerian fire.

America did come to the aid of its closest, cherished, and most important embattled overseas ally after Great Britain was broke. The Grand Alliance was the great moment in the grand story of the English-speaking nations. It does remain Churchillian in the inherited grandeur of its narrative. And America did come to the rescue of England, and together—with enormous although unloved assistance from the Red Army of the Soviet Union and Josef Stalin—America did save the world from the horrors of the Nazis. But while we were gearing up to come to the rescue, we squeezed the British: After all, business is business and power is power, and it is difficult, if not impossible, for an American president to override business and congressional views and powers.

No relationship between the embattled, beleaguered, waning, and indebted once-dominant power and the newly dominant power was ever friendlier, closer, smoother, less conflict-ridden, and all-in-all nicer than the "special relationship" between the United States and Great Britain. Nevertheless, America squeezed the money out. When World War II was over, the United States, not Britain, had the money. When the British borrowed money from us, it had to be repaid in dollars, not in sterling. And imports into Britain had to be rationed well into the 1950s.

Will the United States be similarly squeezed? No. We are not engaged in a total war. We are not desperately in need of military supplies from foreign nations. We do not domestically produce only 1,200 calories of food per citizen per day. We are still by far the world's largest national economy. The United States is technologically powerful and resourceful and is still the center of world finance. World finance is still transacted in dollars. And the United States remains the world's only military superpower, whatever that may turn out to mean.

But the United States is losing the money. America is now massively in debt to foreigners and will be more in debt with each passing year as far into the future as forecasters can see. It will not be similarly squeezed—not squeezed anywhere near as crushingly as Britain—but it will be constrained.

Back when the United States had the money, it used it to pay attention to other governments only when it chose and to make certain that other governments paid attention to the United States even when they wished to not so choose. With the Marshall Plan, America made Western Europe an offer that all but forced Western Europe to adopt the mixed-economy social-democratic order of the post–World War II North Atlantic. America felt itself to be so unchallengeably rich and powerful that it permitted the Japanese to hold down the value of the yen for a generation and rebuild their economy on the basis of exports of industrial products into the United States— even at the eventual expense of American industries such as steel, shipbuilding, automobiles, and machine tools. This was a bearable cost of Cold War–era global leadership.

The United States helped finance the electoral fortunes of democratic forces in some European democracies challenged by what the American government saw as threats to those democracies and to their place in America's liberal world order. The United States financed and arranged "regime change" in lesser countries to remove governments that seemed to be veering off into serious error. With pointed intimations that the United States might pull the financial plug, Dwight D. Eisenhower forced Britain and France to abandon their last colonial intervention in Egypt in 1956. In all this, the United States used the leverage of having the money exclusively for the global greater good.

Who has the money now? What can they do with it? What are they holding? The smallest big batch of money held by other people is simply cash: greenbacks. Perhaps $450 billion, perhaps more, circulates abroad in cash, in hundred-dollar bills. Though not often discussed in polite company, seigniorage, that is, the ability to coin or print cash (the right held by a feudal seigneur) and have other folks hold it, is valuable: Those who hold the hundred-dollar bills have, for many, many years, been providing a substantial loan to the U.S. government— and it's interest free!

Some countries have formally gone over to a dollar economy: "dollarization." Panama is one; Ecuador is another. In other countries (such as Lebanon), cash dollars are widely used. Then, of course, many individuals and organizations prefer the anonymous convenience of hundred-dollar bills: drug dealers; arms merchants; Russian operators; Argentines and Eastern

Europeans with doubts about their local currency; rich and not-so-rich Chinese, who live in a cash economy where the largest Chinese currency note in circulation is one hundred yuan (about fifteen dollars); and people everywhere who like the idea of having some money portable and out of the sight and control of their government (or their spouse's divorce lawyers). And the fact that there are so many cash dollars out there makes each one work all the better. Though the Norwegian krone is a strong currency, you cannot just peel off some kroner somewhere in South America and pay for your hotel room, and when you exchange kroner at a bank, you get clipped because the volume exchanged is small. Furthermore, the cash dollar is secure: When the United States began to issue new hundred-dollar bills with improved anticounterfeiting properties, it did not recall the old bills; instead, the Federal Reserve assured the world that the old notes would continue to be universally accepted, as they are.

The dollar is running into some competition in this business: The biggest cash dollar note in widespread circulation is the one hundred, while the euro has 200-euro and 500-euro denominations in wide circulation, making holding and transporting serious amounts of cash easier. The United States has been reluctant to issue a larger denomination note. Despite a tenfold rise in prices since World War II, the United States has not issued bigger-denomination dollar notes. Cash dollars held abroad constitute one relatively small, steady, and, for the U.S. government, untroubling component of foreign holdings of U.S. obligations: the cheapest loan in the world.

The bigger big batches of dollar-denominated and U.S.-located assets—and they are very big indeed—are not cash

but are rather investments. A great deal is held by private foreign individuals and organizations: Japanese housewives, German doctors, Scottish pension funds, Dutch companies,
Colombian drug lords, Japanese insurance companies, sons of
Gulf sheiks, and Russian "businessmen." Much of the money
is masked: As of June 2007, the Cayman Islands was home to
accounts holding almost $740 billion—$16 million per resident.
In one-dollar bills, that amount would carpet the place to a
luxuriant depth. Tiny Luxembourg is home to another $703
billion.

This money is private money. It belongs to market players—people, companies, organizations, and institutions looking
for the highest returns at the lowest risk. When international
financial transactions are all arms-length market exchanges
between market-oriented players, it doesn't matter much who
has the money or where they live. But private wealth-seeking
individuals are not the entire game, and in fact they never
were. In emergencies, private-market actors always find that
their money, especially foreign holdings, is not under their
control but under the control of its political masters, and theirs:
government. Or it may simply be taken by the foreign government in whose economy it is placed. Even the government
of the United States, for example, confiscated private German
holdings in the United States in 1917 and, of course, again a
generation later.

Much of the money is in the hands of the governments and
rulers of oil-producing states (or in the hands of whatever or
whoever holds their money). Truly great piles of U.S. obligations are in the hands of the governments of Asia. Japan holds

about $1 trillion in reserves (which comes to almost $9,000 per U.S. household). Taiwan, Hong Kong, and Singapore together hold something like $500 billion. Korea sits on another $200 billion.

THE UNITED STATES AND CHINA

China is the biggest holder of U.S. obligations, with some $2.5 trillion in "reserves," the lion's share of it in U.S. debt obligations. Those funds are under political control and direction not just in emergencies but in their normal day-to-day operations.

Should we care? Does it matter? Proverbs 22:7 instructs us: "The borrower is servant to the lender." But the lesson requires some exegesis to fit smoothly into context. The burden of the U.S. foreign debt may be better explained by the oft-repeated Wall Street wisecrack, which we repeat: When you owe the bank $1 million, the bank has got you; when you owe the bank $1 billion, you've got the bank. America doesn't owe money to a big lender who has lots of loans, some of them possibly bigger, to other folks: America owes unimaginably large amounts of money to lenders (such as China), about $20,000 per American household, three-fourths of China's GDP, a fact worth repeating, a fact that makes rapid repayment impossible, leaving aside, for the moment, the brain-twisting transfer-problem question of what form such a payback could conceivably take that would not be ruinous to the Chinese economy. Neither side can walk away; we're locked.

The debt binds China especially and other governments that have the money. Selling the debt would send the dollar

way down and thereby destroy the value of their dollar holdings and severely damage their economies' massive export-
based sectors. Worse yet, sell it for what? Their "reserves"
are so huge that there is nothing else they can hold them in,
not at that scale. They could, and very well might, exchange
their dollar debt obligations for equity: Debt/equity swaps
were all the rage recently. The creditor governments could
buy shares in American companies; there are more than enough
available. Companies on the New York Stock Exchange are
in total worth about $15 trillion—even tossing in GM and Citi
for free—and there is a comparable capital value listed on
NASDAQ. After the stunning fall in these values, some hesi-
tation might be expected. But China and the others will, eventually, buy in and buy out. They could, of course, just spend
their dollars buying U.S. goods and services more and more
each year. Send another hundred thousand Chinese kids to
American universities at full tuition; send thousands and thousands of Chinese tourists to visit New York and California;
buy American products, even some that are not made in
China—but the Chinese probably plan to manufacture those
products soon. Such spending of the dollars would, of course,
rebalance trade flows with the Chinese and others buying
much, much more of American-made goods. That would be
by far the best solution: more actual value for the Chinese and
more employment and less debt for Americans. The opposite
flow of trade—whereby the United States bought from China
and the rest of the world much more than it sold—resulted in
the accumulation of U.S. dollars abroad. But as long as China
wishes to avoid that solution and just hold the dollars as "re-

serves," China now has no alternative. From a Chinese viewpoint, it's exasperating.

Luo Ping, director general at the China Banking Regulatory Commission, put it clearly and vividly: "Except for U.S. Treasuries, what can you hold? . . . For everyone, including China, it is the only option." As the *Financial Times* reported: "Mr. Luo, whose English tends toward the colloquial, added: 'We hate you guys. Once you start issuing $1 trillion–$2 trillion . . . we know the dollar is going to depreciate, so we hate you guys but there is nothing much we can do.'"

The U.S.-China economic imbalance has forced the two powers into a very intimate and not very desired embrace, something Lawrence Summers once called a financial balance of terror. This is all to the good: The two powers must learn to work as partners, and not just in economic matters—global warming and global order also need positive Sino-American cooperation, and they are much more important long-term issues. Despite claims by globalization enthusiasts that strong economic interdependency, such as cross investments and sales, leads to peaceful relations between countries, historically that has not been the case. At the dawn of the twentieth century, Britain, the leading world power, was challenged economically and militarily by a rising power, Germany. Economic ties were deep and strong. Never before and not again until about the year 2000 had there been such globalization (at the time best understood as trade and investment within Europe and North America). In his 1910 book *The Great Illusion,* Norman Angell

argued that war was not a rational option between such economically interdependent neighbors as Britain, France, Austria,
and Germany and that therefore, war would not happen. He
was half right: War proved to be insane. Sino-American part-
nership, in managing the complex mess of their imbalanced
economic codependency, can constitute a good beginning for
managing the utterly unhinged problems of world balance
and order. We have no acceptable choice but to get good at it,
and that will take some doing on both sides.

America knows that it cannot always act "rationally," in
the sense of taking important decisions in insulation from, or
in the face of, the forces of special interests or broad populism;
sometimes it seems that we don't even try. Though it genuinely
deplores the idea, the United States luxuriates in thinking that
the decidedly nondemocratic Chinese government can act rationally with little concern for popular opinion or for the
growth of opposition factions with less dedication to strategic
principles and a greater willingness to fan domestic populism.
The United States makes this assumption at its own peril as
well as its own comfort. China's leadership is acutely sensitive—
some of the most serious American analysts of Chinese politics
say that they are scared stiff of popular indignation and populist
mobilization around themes such as "Why do we lend those
rich Americans all that money? There are better uses for it
here, at home, like health care for me." The new interdependency pressures each side to help the other to act rationally
and accommodate its own failures while striving itself to avoid
or contain populist outbursts, to minimize frictions, even to
cooperate.

As money alters power relations, the United States is not simply becoming dependent—but it is no longer independent, either. That is a major change. And China is no longer helpless and cowed in face of the superpower hegemon; it has got a grip on it. Indeed, while the world peeks in, the two countries are realizing that they have thrown themselves into an intimate economic embrace with, to say the least, very mixed feelings.

Are we at the beginning of the G-2? No. China's economy is still something like one-fifth to one-fourth that of the United States (depending on how it is measured) and smaller than Japan's, not to mention Europe's. And China is still a poor country: GDP per capita lies somewhere between one-fifteenth and one-seventh that of the United States (again, depending upon how it is measured—nominal or PPP [purchasing power parity]).

SOVEREIGN WEALTH AND OTHER PUBLIC ACCUMULATIONS

The coming of large, government-owned asset pools—the result of money flowing in from natural resources, export-driven trade surpluses in manufacturing, and "lemon socialism"— posed a problem for policy makers in the days of the neoliberal dream. The whole point was to get the state's nose out of the economy. Yet here were governments owning large amounts of wealth. And with ownership comes the right to receive the cash flows generated through the profits of businesses. And with a share of profits must come a share of control.

In the United States, there had been an earlier round of discussions and debates focused on the role to be played by the pension funds of government workers—California Public Employees' Retirement System (CalPERS), for example. Were these funds to be used exclusively to earn profits that then would boost the value of the pensions of government workers or diminish the extent to which those promised pensions had to be funded by higher taxes in the future? Or were these funds free to be used for "socially targeted" investments, in which the government would try both to do well for its pensioners and to do good for the economy as a whole by investing the funds in socially targeted enterprises that promised both high rates of return and significant positive economic spillovers?

It looks as though socially targeted investment was mostly a mistake. Experience has shown that diverting attention from market return to social benefit often involved very large financial sacrifices on the part of the pension account and produced little or nothing in the way of faster economic growth. American local governments especially are simply not set up to run successful regional industrial and development policies. Better to narrowly focus government-managed public pension funds on their fiduciary obligations to the ultimate pension recipients. Even though the funds were owned and controlled by governmental entities, they should be managed as if they were not— as if they were just the property of yet another self-interested, profit-maximizing investor seeking risk-adjusted returns.

The basic issue turned out to be much broader. At the start of the 1970s, Peter F. Drucker, management consultant, social theorist, and heir to the Austrian school of social democracy, did the math on the accumulation of pension fund wealth by, or rather on behalf of, the high-paid, high-productivity union-ized manufacturing workers. He found that the projected ac-cumulation of pension fund wealth was absolutely immense, and he forecast a future in 1980 or 1990 in which America would become a country of "pension fund socialism." Socialism would, he thought, emerge not because of the expropriation of the expropriators but rather because of the purchase of shares by (or rather on behalf of) workers from the heirs of capitalists. The working class would simply out-accumulate the capitalist class.

Once pension fund accounts reached critical mass, there would be powerful consequences for corporate control. Union leaders, workers, and their pension fund managers would not be happy with Treasury debt, agency, or AAA bond returns: They would want higher returns from riskier bonds and eq-uities as well. But return and risk require control or at least voice. Pension funds would then be forced to become "active investors," voting slates of managers in and out and seeking and obtaining representation on corporate boards. And then the question would arise: How should all the representatives of all the pension funds administered for the benefit of all the members of the AFL-CIO vote? Should each subfund try hard to redistribute income from the workers they employed to the workers their particular pension was intended to benefit? Or were there gains to the union movement as a whole in pursuing a different strategy?

Drucker was certain that America was going to see pension fund management goals shift toward those of the union move-ment as a whole rather than those of the particular workers to whose retirement the money was committed. In Drucker's view, it would make a real difference when a corporate board had enough members who saw themselves as stewards of the union movement as a whole. Drucker was completely wrong.

Part of it was that the workers who owned the pension funds turned out to be different from the workers who worked for the companies that the pension funds owned. What does a fifty-five-year-old white male in Ypsilanti, Michigan, have in common with a thirty-year-old Latina working in Toluca Lake, California? The rapid fall in union density in the 1970s, 1980s, and 1980s—and the shift out of manufacturing so that the growing unions were those that did not already have large pension fund accumulations—meant that whatever class solidarity might have existed was overwhelmed by generational, regional, and sectoral divides.

But the decisive factor was that legal and institutional structures—laws, regulations, binding court decisions—tamed the funds and forced them into strictly fiduciary behavior. Pension funds could not become a powerful weapon that unions could use in their struggles for higher wages and better working conditions.

There is a key difference between then and now. Then—with the rise of pension funds within the United States—the government set and controlled the rules of the game. A president, a Congress, and a legal system that did not want workers' investments to carry with them workers' "ownership" in the sense of control over enterprises could and did block developments in that direction. Today, the rules are different: The rule is that there are no rules—we are still in the Westphalian anarchy of international relations. Any demand by a host country that the Chinese, French, Korean, or Saudi government should confine itself in the deployment of its wealth to merely seeking the highest risk-adjusted expected return will be not a command or a demand but a request. And whether that request will be honored depends on what two governments, one of which has the money, negotiate rather than on what one government commands. And there is no routine policing.

In the deployment of U.S. pension fund money in the past two generations, the fact that there was a single government setting the rules was an overwhelmingly powerful factor. As a result, the legal duties of a fiduciary—to be a money manager and only a money manager—had enormous consequences. And just because unionized workers had bargained for and in some sense owned their pension fund reserves did not mean that union officials in any sense controlled or had influence over them—at least not in well-run unions. (The Teamsters in Las Vegas were a somewhat different story.)

As the holdings of sovereign wealth funds and their cousins burgeoned in the early 2000s, the same forces that had focused union pension funds on the narrowly economic deployed to tame sovereign wealth funds. The intellectual lead was taken by Edwin Truman, a senior economist at the Peterson Institute for International Economics. Truman was also a former assistant secretary of the Treasury for International Affairs and a former director of the Federal Reserve's Division of International Finance. The idea was to develop a "code of conduct" for sovereign wealth funds. Governments should commit to making their sovereign wealth fund accumulations transparent, to devolving their portfolio management to financial-sector professionals, and to making the goal of the portfolio managers that of being good market and exclusively market actors—to maximize risk-adjusted asset returns rather than to pursue broader goals of national economic development or of political leverage.

As long as the tide was flowing in the neoliberal direction, Truman and company had a good chance and a good case. Concessions on the sovereign wealth fund front—agreements to take part in the development of an arm's-length code of conduct and then moves toward following that code of conduct in the governance of one's own sovereign wealth funds—could provide tasty appetizers at the banquet of increasing globalization. In a world in which the big international economic issues involved the removal of nontariff barriers, the continued expansion of world trade, the promotion of global technology transfer, and the use of international institutions to manage and control systemic risk, to agree to work to wall off sovereign wealth fund accumulations from "political" considerations was an ante that got one into the game of expanding globalization. And in this game, the pot promised to be very large indeed.

But the financial crisis that began in 2007 is shattering the neoliberal dream. The presumption that the great and good of Washington know how governments should manage political economy is out the window. The pot from the global neoliberal game has grown smaller. And the value of the ante committed by agreeing to a broadly neoliberal code of conduct on sovereign wealth funds appears to be larger.

Thus, the way to bet right now is that the neoliberal dream is largely over. Sovereign wealth fund portfolio management will not be focused on maximizing risk-adjusted returns alone. It will matter that sovereign wealth funds are the investment instruments of governments rather than of the world's private-sector well-off.

How it will matter is not yet clear. But that it will matter, is. And to understand how it will matter, we need to go back to 1945 and track the coming, the hold, and the awakening from the neoliberal dream.

THREE

What the Dream Had Been

One way to understand the neoliberal dream of the 1990s and early 2000s is that it was based on the assertion that government had a narrow range of core activities in which it was competent (or at least less incompetent than other institutions)—establishing property rights, adjudicating disputes, managing monetary policy, providing social insurance, building infrastructure, and providing other public goods such as defense and water projects—and a set of activities in which it was incompetent: everything else. For the neoliberals, the shrinking of the sphere of state action back to its core competencies was a very important task (although it had not been for the generation after World War II).

THE MIXED ECONOMY

For the first generation after World War II, it was accepted that the government would have a very large and multifaceted role in the economy. Economics textbooks no longer spoke of capitalism or a market economy as if those were unalloyed good things. We lived, they assured us, in a mixed economy— an economy that avoided the ham-handed deficiencies and inefficiencies of top-down bureaucratic central planning, but also an economy in which the invisible hand of the market was supported and aided by the very visible hands of the government. This economy was structured at its core by solid institutions: big unions and large, stable oligopolistic firms with a good deal of control over the prices they charged, and regulation was pervasive. The mixed economy thus avoided the destruction and waste of Great Depressions through activist fiscal and monetary policies to keep manufacturing production near capacity, total demand near to the economy's productive potential, and employment nearly full. It also reduced the waste caused by market failure: the diversion of resources to enterprises that market prices rewarded at more than their social value—and the lost opportunities and waste that arose from market failures that kept markets from functioning well. Different industrialized North Atlantic countries followed different individual paths, but they were all mixed economies.

Some were less successful. The British Labour Party government of Clement Attlee had nationalized the "commanding heights" of the economy, British Rail, British Coal, British Steel, and so on—the real lemons—in the immediate aftermath of World War II. These nationalized industries could, they thought, realize immense economies of scale like those of the firms of the continent-spanning United States—economies of scale that could not be achieved in an industry divided among competing firms on a small island. They also had the theoretical advantage that government-run industries did not have to cover their fixed costs by charging high prices. Instead, they could boost economic growth and demand for their products by reducing their prices to the economically efficient level of marginal cost, with general tax revenues filling the hole. That meant cheaper steel and cheaper railroad tickets. Patient and public-spirited governments could, in theory, invest in the future of these industries in a wise and farsighted manner that would produce a better outcome than would funding by private capital markets subject to fits of enthusiasm and depression and always impatient for cash flows. While a private company might want to wring out profits from a railroad quarter by fiscal quarter, the government could take a longer view and preserve an important industry that served a large part of its citizens (or subjects). Government control of these industries also meant that wage bargaining between one group of the people and the people as a whole (that is, the government) would be much less acrimonious than wage bargaining between salt-of-the-earth workers and managers working for rich upper-class twits born with silver spoons in their mouths.

wrong?

All of these claimed benefits turned out to be wrong.

With the British approach to a mixed economy, standards of living and levels of productivity on the island fell behind those across the English Channel. Britain had long ago come to terms with the idea that the United States would be richer and more prosperous with its greater natural resources and the efficiencies of a continent-spanning market—that, in the words of economic historian J. H. Clapham, it was in the long run inevitable that "a continent would . . . raise more coal and make more steel than one small island." But the widening gap with France, Holland, and Belgium was more troubling to behold. The political logic of running a nationalized industry ran counter to the economic logic. It made the anticipated economies of scale hard to actually achieve: Some region's plant had to be closed down, which meant that some member of Parliament's unionized constituents had to be fired. This proved difficult, especially under a British Labour government. Pressure for expansion of social insurance and state services ensured that the British Treasury was never happy to increase the subsidy to the nationalized firms of the "commanding heights." Indeed, the reverse was more common: The investment funds of the nationalized industries were easy targets to raid whenever a Chancellor of the Exchequer wanted to hold the line on taxes in his next budget speech, so the capital equipment aged. And labor relations between unions and the government—even when the unions had played a big role in choosing which Labour Party politicians would be the government—were if anything worse than they had been before.

For other countries, such as France, economists were pessimistic, even disparaging. As late as 1958, a RAND Corporation study portrayed France as an economic sick man. It was politically dysfunctional: France ran through twenty-seven prime ministers (some repeats) between 1946 and 1958. It was economically handicapped: These revolving-door governments commanded a hypertrophic state apparatus that was the most centralized, the most interventionist, and the most pervasively involved in the economy of any nation that sought to be taken seriously. Economic historian David Landes explained that the family tradition of French capitalism was hostile to expansion and thus to efficiency. The political power of the peasantry who had gained ownership of their small farms when they burned the rolls listing their feudal obligations to the nobility in the summer of 1789 produced a large bloc hostile to the provision of the infrastructure needed for a modern urban economy. The ideological hegemony that the Stalinist Communist Party of France exercised over the industrial workers of northern France and the Paris suburbs ensured that a large chunk of both wage bargaining and voting was directed by people who would rather see the French economy fail than succeed. The state dominated industry and pretty much the rest of the economy both by ownership—the French state had taken ownership of more commanding heights than even Britain had—and by the pervasiveness of its regulations, controls, and interventions.

Nevertheless, or perhaps because of all that, the rather statist French version of the mixed economy was astonishingly successful in spurring economic growth and modernization. GDP grew at an average rate of 4.4 percent from 1950 to 1958—admittedly, the period can be seen as the years of easy growth through reconstruction and catch-up, but France was growing almost twice as fast as Britain, which faced a similar set of challenges, and far faster than the United States, which had nothing to reconstruct and no one to catch up to. Then, between 1958 and 1964, French growth accelerated to 5.4 percent, keeping pace with the ever-disciplined, hardworking Germans.

The inability of any prime minister and his government to stay in power for more than a few months left the responsibility for minding the store to the elite, technocratic bureaucracy—the real architects of France's industrial development. And, of course, France moved the peasants off the farm—slowly, respectfully, intergenerationally. Farmers' children left for higher-value-added jobs in the cities and towns. About one-third of the French population was involved in agriculture at the war's end, while only about 3.5 percent is now, and many of today's "farmers" are Parisian cosmetic surgeons who keep some fruit trees, horses, and cows for aesthetic and tax purposes.

The French were not the only mixed-economy champions. It came as a surprise to many—especially the Italians—that Italy, with a spectacularly dysfunctional government, with a south that was not part of prewar or even postwar industrial Europe, and with a gigantic state-owned sector, managed to grow in the 1950s and 1960s considerably faster than Britain or the United States.

Today we think of the American economy as one that, save for Roosevelt's New Deal, has always been a free-enterprise economy, a market economy, an economy where people test themselves and their skills against the market and their competitors and emerge either rich if they are lucky, smart, and hardworking; middle-class if their lack of big-time luck is offset by prudence, thrift, and industry; or poor if they are imprudent, unenterprising, and unable to resist the temptations of the Vegas Strip or the $5,000-limit-with-2-percent-interest-for-the-first-six-months credit card. The government stands on the sidelines as umpire. The public schools teach you the basic skills and the rules; the Department of Health and Human Services provides a modest safety net; Congress spends money on national defense, scientific research, courts, and essential infrastructure; and there are a few high-level technocratic and technical economic-stabilization tasks performed by government that nobody but Ben Bernanke or Alan Greenspan really understands—but otherwise, you get out there and play by yourself.

This has never been an accurate picture of America. And in the generation after World War II, it was less accurate than usual.

The United States followed its own road to the mixed economy. American politics was averse to government ownership of enterprises. But American politics was not averse to having the government spend big on defense; build infrastructure, mostly roads and bridges; and guarantee debts. The creation of the great government-sponsored mortgage companies—Fannie Mae and Freddie Mac—greatly multiplied the ability of middle-class families to back their long-held dream of a suburban house of their own with borrowed cash (insured by the government).

The U.S. government did not, like the French, practice "indicative planning." It did not regularly suggest to the executives of GM and DuPont and Bethlehem Steel that they might want to invest on such-and-such a scale in such-and-such a market segment to make such-and-such a set of products. What the U.S. government did do was to put cash down on the barrelhead: There was a Cold War to be fought, after all, and the Cold War demanded arming to the teeth against the Russkies—with peacetime defense spending levels passing 9 percent of GDP, much of that invested in and producing what were for the time the highest of high-tech products.

Those investments turned out to have dual uses. The jet aircraft assembly lines of Boeing got their start building warplanes and were only later repurposed to serve civilian commercial demand. The first computers were for the Bureau of the Census and for the SAGE air-defense system and only later for private-sector use. The U.S. government also shaped market outcomes through its pervasive regulatory activities. The government-sponsored mortgage market was one of two government policies—the other was archly named the National Defense Highway Act that created the enormous burst in suburbanization that shaped not only the American landscape but the sectoral composition of the economy. The highways and houses necessitated automobiles, which drank oil (in those days it came from Texas, not the Persian Gulf). Government policies had a direct impact on a broad range of sectors. Government granted TV broadcasters their broadcast frequencies for free. Airlines got a dense network of airports and regulated fares; truckers got their highways and regulations to tame price competition (which also protected freight railways). Stockbrokers got noncompetitive commissions; bankers got deposit insurance, regulations on prudential investment, and banker hours; textile mills got import quotas. And America got the closest ever to steady full employment and a steady 2.5 percent annual increase in productivity, which doubled real average income every twenty-five years.

Combine military demand with mortgage guarantees, add on funds for interstate highways and airports, include a progressive tax system and state and local governments focused on increasing access to education, control with extensive regulation, and cap it all off with expansionary fiscal and monetary policies—and you have an American mixed economy that looks different from those of continental Europe or Great Britain, has little government ownership, has fewer bureaucratic sticks and regulatory dikes, and has more carrots. But is not in any sense a smaller or a less comprehensive set of governmental interventions in the economy. That was the state of play over the entire North Atlantic region—in the United States as well as in Western Europe—up into the second half of the 1970s, at the end of the first post–World War II generation.

THE ROLLBACK OF THE MIXED ECONOMY

The mixed economy had always had its enemies in America. In 1960, Senator Barry Goldwater of Arizona—who would be the 1964 Republican presidential nominee and who had just cast the last vote he would ever cast for a civil rights bill—denounced it as "one of the great evils of Welfarism . . . that it transforms the individual from a dignified, industrious, self-reliant spiritual being into a dependent animal creature without his knowing it."

For Goldwater and his followers, the idea that one should try to make the government cost-effective in its functions was simply beside the point: "I have little interest in streamlining government or making it more efficient, for I mean to reduce its size. I do not undertake to promote welfare, for I propose to extend freedom. My aim is not to pass laws, but to repeal them."

Perhaps the enemies of the mixed economy were not as clear-sighted or as straight-talking as they thought. Presumably, the laws that would be repealed did not include those that gave the government guarantee to the mortgages that funded the houses of southern Arizona. Nor would the repealed laws include those that funded the projects that brought water for drinking, washing, and lawn-sprinkling in the Arizona desert from the rivers originating in the Rocky Mountains or the laws that built the highways of southern Arizona, on which the customers of Goldwater's Department Store drove. Reduce the size of the government too far, and Goldwater's Department Store—indeed, all of Phoenix—literally dries up and blows away.

But there were more sophisticated critics in America in the 1960s and 1970s who held that we had built the wrong kind of mixed economy and that the state had exceeded its proper bounds and was taking on missions that it could not accomplish efficiently at all. Moreover, as critics like University of Maryland economist Mancur Olson argued, the private sector had an automatic sunset mechanism that the government did not: The government-run portion of the mixed economy would become increasingly institutionally sclerotic over time and would need some sort of purging of bureaucratic inefficiency. In addition, there was the danger of corruption by interest groups that found it easy to mobilize politically to lobby the democratic process. From one popular perspective in the 1970s, the mixed economy was in reality an arrangement by which big labor and big business paid big money to buy influence peddlers and seize control of big government, which then shafted the rest of us.

From this viewpoint sprang the deregulation movement of the 1960s and 1970s, initially pushed by technocrats who wished to see the mixed economy function more efficiently. Economist Charles Schultze, at the head of President Lyndon Johnson's Bureau of the Budget, pushed through the "privatization" of Fannie Mae and Freddie Mac. He argued that they were now large enough and the mortgage market thick and deep enough that they did not need their government guarantee for the mortgage market to function. Moreover, their possession of a government guarantee kept them fat, inefficient, and lazy, giving them an unfair competitive advantage over would-be private-sector competitors. And finally, the government-sponsored enterprises (GSEs) were pushing America toward a suburban geography in which the government's thumb was making it too cheap for too many Americans to own and live in their own suburban homes. (In the short run, Schultze succeeded: Fannie Mae and Freddie Mac were privatized, so that the profits went not to the government but to shareholders, executives, and politicians who received campaign contributions. In the long run, he failed: Everyone continued to believe that the GSEs had a government guarantee, so the government's thumb remained on the mortgage market. And indeed, in 2008, when the two companies went bust, it turned out that they still did have a government guarantee.)

Economist Alfred Kahn, working for President Jimmy Carter, argued for the deregulation of airlines and trucking. The Interstate Commerce Commission, which had been established to protect the farmer against the monopolistic railroad, instead now protected the railroad against the more efficient trucking company (running on subsidized interstate highways)—and in the process wound up taxing the American consumer for the benefit of the members of the Teamsters' Union. The original allocation of scarce landing slots at publicly built airports by the Federal Aviation Administration and the imposition of fare controls had created a situation in which many too few people paid much too much for airline tickets and flew on airplanes that had much too much in the way of luxury because airlines were forbidden to compete on the more natural dimension of price. Deregulation was, however, a fringe technocratic good-government movement. And it would have in all probability remained a fringe technocratic good-government movement were it not for the macroeconomic breakdown of the 1970s.

The 1970s saw both the first large, sustained, peacetime worldwide episode of notable (but not disastrous) inflation and the worst recessions (then) of the post–World War II era, culminating in the worldwide "Volcker Deep Recession." For the first time since World War II, the possibility that you might become and remain unemployed for years became something to weigh in the calculations of every voter in all of the North Atlantic democracies. And for the first time ever in peacetime, uncertainty about the future level of prices made every business decision a speculation on monetary policy.

In magnitude, the total increase in the price level as a result of the sustained spurt in peacetime inflation to an annual 5 to 10 percent range in the 1970s was no larger than the jumps that came about as a result of World War I and World War II—jumps that were accepted at the time and contained afterward. But we were not at war, and so the political consequences proved much more disruptive.

Each temporary surge in inflation was quickly followed by—or in the case of the mid-1970s oil-shock inflation cycle, roughly coincident with—an increase in unemployment. Each cycle in the late 1960s and 1970s was larger than the one before: Unemployment peaked at around 6 percent in 1971, at about 8.5 percent in 1975, and at nearly 10 percent in 1982–1983. When Congress attempted to legislate full employment, Federal Reserve chair Arthur Burns pushed back:

> [The] Humphrey-Hawkins [proposal] . . . continues the old game of setting a target for the unemployment rate. You set one figure. I set another figure. If your figure is low, you are a friend of mankind; if mine is high, I am a servant of Wall Street. . . . I think that is not a profitable game.

In a sense, the truest cause of the 1970s inflation was the shadow of the Great Depression. The memory left by the Depression predisposed the left and center to think that any unemployment was too much; such thinking eliminated any mandate the Federal Reserve might have had for controlling inflation by risking unemployment. The result was that any big upward shock to prices—like the oil shocks of 1973 and 1979—would automatically set off an upward spiral of inflation that could be stopped only at a cost that the Federal Reserve did not think it had a mandate to impose on the economy. During the 1970s, as discontent built over that decade's inflation, the Federal Reserve gained, or regained, such a mandate to control inflation at the risk of unemployment. Thus, the memory of the Great Depression meant that the United States was highly likely to suffer an inflation like the 1970s in the post–World War II period—maybe not as long, and maybe not in that particular decade, but nevertheless an inflation of recognizably the same genus.

The political consequences of the inflation of the 1970s and its associated recessions were mighty.

The diagnosis of the economic problem that the Thatcher-led Conservatives carried into power in Britain and the Reagan-led Republicans carried into power in the United States at the end of the 1970s had two parts. First, the United States in the late 1970s had a high rate of both inflation and unemployment because the Federal Reserve had been too soft and too unwilling to understand that some unemployment was a necessity of modern capitalism.

The new prescription was to accept whatever unemployment was necessary to attain price stability. The new (1979) Federal Reserve chair, Paul Volcker, and his open-market committee were consequently given free rein to raise unemployment to fight inflation. The belief was that an economy in which workers believed that they could not price themselves out of a job, no matter how hard they bargained, was an unsustainable economy.

The second part of the diagnosis was that not just the Federal Reserve but also the whole government had been too soft. The government needed to provide less social insurance and run far fewer programs. As conservative Republican economist Martin Feldstein put it:

> Expansionary policies were adopted in the hope of lowering the unemployment rate but without anticipating

the inflation. High tax rates on investment income were enacted and social security retirement benefits were increased without considering the subsequent impact on investment and saving. Regulations were imposed to protect health and safety without evaluating the reduction in productivity that would result or the effect of an uncertain regulatory future on long-term [activities]. [T]he government never considered that [high] unemployment benefits would encourage layoffs; that Medicare and Medicaid might lead to an explosion in health care costs; that welfare programs to help [the] poor might weaken family structures; or that federal aid through the tax laws to encourage [suburban] homeownership would have such adverse effects on the cities, precipitating relocation of businesses [to the suburbs] and [creating] poverty and other problems for those left behind.

The perception that there were substantial flaws in the social-democratic fabric of the mixed economy was not wrong. Why, in Britain, did education policy turn out to give children of doctors and lawyers the right to go to Oxford without paying for it? The sociologist T. H. Marshall had looked forward to an extension of the concept of equal rights to equal social and economic rights: the right to work, the right to an education, the right to a fair and equal share of what society can produce. But this extension stalled: The rollback began. The failure of the managers of the mixed economy to produce full employment and price stability in the 1970s undermined the whole enterprise—and created the opportunity for the neoliberals to attempt to implement their dream.

NEOLIBERAL UTOPIA

The hope of the neoliberals was to cut the government down to its core functions and so to build something much more like a utopia by avoiding the political haggling, the legal corruption, the illegal corruption, the bureaucratic inefficiencies, and the destructive impact of the social-democratic mixed-economy welfare state on the incentives and the morals of bosses and workers. Government could, neoliberals thought, build infrastructure, administer (possibly progressive) tax systems, fund a safety net, enforce contracts, and possibly add taxes and bounties that would compensate for the most gross externalities and market imperfections. Beyond that, neoliberals from Carter to Clinton argued, government should not go.

Thus, the differences in politico-economic policy between Democrats and Labour Party politicians like Carter, Clinton, Blair, and Brown and their staffs on the one hand and Reagan and Thatcher on the other were not differences in means but rather differences in ends. Those on the left thought that progressive income taxes to redistribute wealth from the rich to the middle class and aggressive uplift programs to promote real equality of opportunity remained a core function of government—and should be amply and generously funded, even at the cost of high marginal tax rates for the rich and potential featherbedding on the part of the poor and the employees of the public sector.

Politicians on the right felt very differently. The money of the rich belonged to the rich, and it was wrong for the government to take it away via progressive taxation. It was wrong even if, say, one thing that put William Gates's Microsoft on IBM's radar screen when Big Blue was recruiting partners for the PC was that Gates had chosen the right parents—his mother had served on the national board of the United Way alongside IBM CEO John F. Akers. And politicians on the right thought that equality of opportunity was not a goal worth pursuing if pursuing it for the young seriously required—as it did—substantial progressive income taxes and an increase in equality of result for the relatively old.

Politicians on the left tended to give a Rawlsian defense that the best way to help the poor was not to punish but to incentivize the rich: Shrinking the regulatory, interventionist, and management role of the states and cutting back on progressive taxes would align the economic incentives of the rich with the social goal of economic growth, and in the end, the relatively poor would wind up better off in a more unequal but much richer society. Politicians on the right tended to regard greater inequality as an absolute virtue: Those at the top of the economic pyramid—because of their smarts, their skills, their enterprise, their industry, their luck, their success at choosing the right parents—deserved a very comfortable life and to be sharply distinguished from their fellow citizens.

Politicians on the left applied further balm to their consciences by hoping that a state with a smaller role would be less corrupt. When he was head of the Office of Management and Budget under Ronald Reagan, David Stockman argued furiously that Washington would always and inevitably be constituted so that the calculus of government would benefit private and not public interests. Those who benefited from government management of the economy would not be those with strong claims to government resources but rather those who were strong claimants—like the Gallo family, whose estate tax liabilities were of concern to sometime Senate Finance Committee Chair Robert Dole even though no Gallo had ever lived in Kansas. To the extent that the executive branch and the legislature of the modern state were nothing but a set of committees for managing the affairs of a rich ruling class, the act of shrinking the arena for state intervention in, and management of, the economy was a profoundly progressive and leveling act.

Center-left politicians, their staffs and advisers, and intellectuals had by 2000 convinced themselves that neoliberalism was thus a more effective means toward achieving social-democratic ends of comfort for the poor and upward mobility for the striving than the social democracy of the post–World War II era. Their belief that there was a difference in kind between operations that the government should avoid entirely and those in which the government should take a mighty role was never fully justified. Economist Dani Rodrik has made his career arguing for social democracy in a neoliberal age, pointing out that this bright line made much less sense than its advocates and true believers maintained. Arguments against government interventions classified as bad "industrial policy," Rodrik maintained, could be equally well or almost equally well deployed against activities that nearly all saw as within the good core sphere of public responsibilities:

> Consider . . . policy interventions targeted on a loosely-
> defined set of market imperfections . . . implemented by

bureaucrats . . . overseen by politicians . . . corruption
and rent-seeking . . . powerful groups and lobbies. . . .
[Y]ou react by saying "these are all reasons why governments should stay away from industrial policy." But . . .
I have in mind . . . education, health, social insurance,
and macroeconomic stabilization. . . . Interventions in
each one of the conventional areas I just listed are justified by market failures that are widely felt to exist, although rarely documented . . . bureaucrats . . . powerful
groups and lobbies. . . . [Yet] debates in these policy areas
are rarely ever about whether the government should
be involved; they are about how. . . . Why can't industrial
policy be the same? It's beyond me.

He never received a satisfactory answer.

There were always two profound exceptions to the logic of
neoliberalism. The first is spending on national defense, including science and technology to support defense where the United
States spends more than the next fifteen countries combined.
The second came in finance—specifically, in central banking.

Back in 1998, *Time* magazine anointed Federal Reserve
Chair Alan Greenspan, Treasury Secretary Robert Rubin, and
Treasury Undersecretary Lawrence Summers the "committee
to save the world." They were not elected heads of government
or the representatives of voters but rather pure technocrats.
Those who did have legitimate executive or legislative authority
derived from the masses by an electoral mandate found that,
in the financial crisis of 1997–1998, their role and power were
reduced to little more than those of the queen of England.

They had the right to be consulted by deciders—Greenspan, Rubin, and Summers—before the deciders acted, they had the right to advise the deciders (to the extent that the politicians understood the issues), and they had the right to warn about the consequences of mistakes and failures. Little more.

For almost all the twentieth century, central bankers have been the closest thing to central economic planners that the industrial democracies of the North Atlantic have ever had. This was almost as true in the 1920s as it has been in the 2000s. Even at the high tide of shrink-the-state neoliberalism, the power of the moral-philosopher-princes who are central bankers only grew and grew. While the idea of social democracy—government ownership, control, and regulation of at least the "commanding heights" of the economy—was in retreat, the strength of this immense island of central planning was on the advance. The Federal Reserve chair in the 1950s and 1960s, William McChesney Martin, deferred to the U.S. president. The Fed chair in the 1970s, Arthur Burns, feared that Congress would amend the Federal Reserve Act, and these fears greatly limited his perception of his freedom of action. But nobody challenges Ben Bernanke or his predecessors Alan Greenspan and Paul Volcker as they decide in normal times what the short-term interest rate is and as they decide in abnormal times which financial institutions shall live and which shall die.

It would be too much of a digression to follow the story of central banker power from it origins in Britain in 1825 and 1844 to the present day. Suffice it to say that today, eight times a year and also in emergencies the Federal Reserve's Federal

Open Market Committee meets in the large conference room on the second floor of the Eccles Building on the Mall in Washington, D.C., to set the level of the federal funds interest rate. The committee keeps an eye, first, to maintaining price stability (because inflation makes all other tasks much more difficult); second, to minimizing the danger of current or future financial crisis; and, third, to keeping the economy's level of growth as high and unemployment as low as possible, given the other two objectives. How to trade off these three objectives is left to the Federal Reserve, and to the Federal Reserve alone. The U.S. Treasury's press release to accompany Federal Reserve decisions is standardized:

> Our role at the Treasury Department is to support the independent regulators. . . . The Treasury Department supports the actions taken by the Federal Reserve Bank of New York and the Federal Reserve. We believe the actions taken were necessary and appropriate.

The Federal Reserve in the United States and independent central banks all over the North Atlantic have their role today as an interventionist fourth branch of the government not by design but by historical happenstance. Whatever the claims of a "market economy," governments at key moments proved unwilling to let markets determine key interest rates and asset prices.

Had we collectively been wiser, the financial crises in Mexico (1994–1995) and East Asia (1997–1998) would have warned us that there was something wrong with the foundations of the neoliberal order. Neoliberalism based itself on the idea that if we could transform the system so that rational, privately interested economic agents faced the correct incentives, then government did not need to step in. But then why the 1994–1995 and 1997–1998 financial crises? As accomplished and as insightful a self-proclaimed Liberal economist as Paul Krugman mused that these episodes revealed "theoretical weaknesses" in economists' view of the world, but then reassured himself that even if neoliberalism was false in theory, it could still be made true or true enough in practice if the technocratic central banks were allowed to use their discretion in the ways that they knew how: "[While] economists have argued with each other over whether [central bank] monetary policy can [theoretically] . . . be used to get an economy out of a recession, central banks have repeatedly gone ahead and used it to do just that—so effectively in fact that the idea of a prolonged economic slump . . . became implausible."

It was this confidence—that only a single island of central planning and government discretionary power in the form of technocratic central banks was needed to provide a sufficient stabilizing balance wheel to make the neoliberal utopia functional—that has come crashing down in the past two years.

MONEY AND CULTURE: SOFT POWER

For the past thirty years, America rather successfully propagated to itself and others a worldview of unfettered markets and "re-fettered" states: Expand the realm of markets in society and roll back the reach of other institutions, especially government. This worldview carried with it a cultural content of primacy of finance (that would have pleased Balzac), of new business practices and styles, and of celebratory income inequality on the consumption and lifestyle side. Until it crashed, this American view was willingly adopted by more and more people and governments around the globe. It was, of course, backed by the certification of money: This is what the money wanted; this is what the money did; and this is what made for more money. To a great and unfortunate extent, the view dominated perceptions of America and American culture.

Money, of course, is power. But money power is not only—not even essentially—about paying people to do your wont. It is about having it and getting more and more of it visibly and legitimately and doing so for a convincingly considerable time. Paying people to do what you want is expensive, and outside the surprisingly restricted realm of straightforward commercial transactions, it is not all that effective. Because America had the money—had it solidly, rightfully, self-assuredly, and durably—for about one hundred years, people all over the world wanted to be like Americans: successful, modern, loose-jointed, efficient, democratic, socially mobile, leggy, clean, powerful, and, of course, rich. It was clearly the way to be. America enjoyed the world's predominant position in soft power, long before and, most likely, long after the wrapping of the American message in the shimmering foil of the neoliberal worldview.

Soft power—not military might, not straight-out money, but the ability to inspire acceptance and imitation—was a vital component of American international dominance. It soothed the abrasiveness of military and economic power and made the wielders of such power feel good.

In the nineteenth century, Britain's upper classes created a myth: a myth that they were the heirs of and the carriers of the tradition of Greek culture, Roman law and order, Jewish fear of the Lord, Medieval chivalry, and native British traditions of limited government and personal cussedness—and they called this *Western civilization*. British economic dominance in the nineteenth century convinced first themselves, and then nearly everyone else, that this "Western civilization" was *the* secret—*the* way—that everybody needed to grasp, copy, and adapt to their purposes. Long after political and economic power shift, the assimilated elements of a nation's cultural dominance endure. Over a century, this worldwide process of grasping, copying, and adapting their ways made a world that was a very comfortable place indeed for the upper-class English to live after the money waved good-bye to Britain. It may even have made for a better world.

In the age of Voltaire, gentlemen fenced (sometimes for real) and rode horses; ordinary folks didn't really need extra exercise. In the age of Victoria, English boarding schools invented Organized Sports, and English schoolboy sports—rugby, cricket, modern tennis, and soccer—spread across the world like railroads, English banking practices, and afternoon tea. So did the dress of English gentlemen.

Voltaire, as much as any single individual, took down the ancien régime. His powerful and popular writings brought rationality—light, as it was then called—to the world of the ancien régime, which much preferred flickering candlelight against a deep background of darkness—far more suitable for its bone structure of faith, myth, and display. But Voltaire did not shun display—not just of his quicksilver mind and personality, but in his clothing as well. Portraits show him in blue and red and green silks and velvets and a powdered white wig, the proper French-inspired attire of the European upper classes. The philosophers of the Enlightenment dressed as brilliantly as they spoke—to the distant eye, rather like Mozart did years earlier.

Like much in the world of ideas, discourse, and comportment, sartorial style radiated outward like the beams of the sun from the power center of agricultural Europe: the royal court at Versailles, which, starting in the seventeenth century, controlled the rents extracted from twenty million French peasants and channeled them into the production of luxuries. Versailles French, the language of the French aristocrats turned courtier   and throughout the eighteenth century, still a foreign language to more than half the French population—was the international language and even the day-to-day language in such self-consciously backward elite circles as the Russian aristocracy. In the eighteenth century, it was French culture that radiated and predominated. In the sixteenth, it was Italian: The economic prowess of Italian cities developed in the fifteenth century meant that sixteenth-century monarchs like England's Henry VIII Tudor were eager to dress like the Italian bankers who lent them money and to eat like them—with the fork. But little of this affected the daily life of most people.

A long and troubled generation after the Enlightenment, gentlemen, first in England and then all over "the civilized world," replaced their bright silks, velvets, and powdered wigs with black or gray suits. The new outfits reflected more the power of Protestant bankers and the drear aura of the counting house than the glittering court of an aristocratic, agricultural society. The black (or gray or pinstriped) suit has had a long run; with minor changes in collars and jacket length and the more complex evolution of the necktie, J. P. Morgan dressed pretty much the same as his fellow bankers did one hundred years earlier and as his successors on Wall Street are doing one hundred years later.

The French Revolution most abruptly changed Paris fashions—remember the *sans culottes*. But it was overwhelmingly the change in English men's fashion that counted. England was now clearly seen as the leading power well on its way to being the economic center of the world. Commerce, industry, ideas, and, of course, money centered on London. Legend has it that Beau Brummell led the way for this transformation at the top of English society. Quickly the rest of the world followed suit.

Money brings a nation power, not just the power to command, or at least influence, the behavior of other nations. And when the money accumulates over time and as a result of real economic success, and not just windfalls from guano or oil deposits, it brings the power to propagate, consciously or not, the ideas, concerns, fashions, norms, interests, amusements, and ways of displaying and behaving that come out of its culture. These penetrate deep down into other cultures as well as its own; they become part of daily life. This is luxuriant power:

Face
of
power

It doesn't have to be exercised willfully or even consciously, and it doesn't even cost anything extra.

As the United States emerged in the aftermath of World War I as the top power and giant money master, American jazz swept through Europe, faster than Ford and Kodak. Later, especially after World War II, Europeans eagerly welcomed the onslaught of American movies. They stared bedazzled at the intimate display of the new American life: rich, different, new, powerful, and rather wonderful, although for some, of dubious cultural value and arguably (which they did enthusiastically) a new form of opium for the masses. Most Europeans encountered America at the movies, but two generations of rather privileged Europeans traveled to America to see for themselves (many sponsored by the State Department), to behold the skyscrapers of New York, the George Washington and Golden Gate bridges, and the houses of rather ordinary people with huge shiny cars, washing machines, televisions, and the orthodontically enhanced smiles on tall, milk-and meat-fed women. Even Jean Paul Sartre marveled at the "great Avenues of New York heading to the West"; he got the essence of the thing right, if not the geography. America overpowered the European literary tradition of the brooding adolescent (*Werther, Tonio Kröger, Le Grand Meaulnes*) with our invention, the teenager, a product—and a motor—of our big cultural-economic invention, the society of mass-consumption individualism. None of those European adolescent romantics busied himself spending; teenagers do. American cultural dominance is twentieth century, though the money surge began in the nineteenth. Until we achieved thoroughgoing economic dominance, we were a nation that was self-consciously provincial in traditional high culture—painting, writing, music, furniture making, cooking and eating, fashion, philosophy, and science.

American cultural dominance has continued to grow. Teenagers around the globe now uniformly dress in styles pioneered by American teens and have even adopted the same body language. They eat on the street. The American-designed, Asian-manufactured iPods fill their heads with the same harsh music; they instant-message, tweak, and twitter. And the English language—not altogether an American cultural invention—is not merely the international language, but also the second language for a vast global population: Languages carry more than their words and grammar; they carry cultural form and content.

America will be less and less the origin of new cultural trends or global memes: First, because the others now have the money. But also, as Gertrude Stein remarked more than half a century ago, "America is the oldest country because we have been modern for so long." The culture we exported—to ourselves and to the world—was our shaping of modernity. We were the first to modernize. But the culture of modernization, somewhat different from modernity itself, can age quickly because it implies relentless novelty and especially the energetic creations of a society organizing around the practice and celebration of the mass consumption.

America remains especially modern, but the modern is no longer especially American; it is rapidly becoming semiglobal and if not old, at least very mature. There is no need to leave China to see skyscrapers; there are more of them in Shanghai

than in New York, and they are newer, taller and bolder. The
energy—that key element in New York 1920s literature (e.g.,
Dos Passos) has, with the money, shifted its residence. Even
Las Vegas, a quintessentially American cultural invention—
no European would ever have thought of it—has gone global:
Macau rivals Las Vegas in the brazenness of its casinos and
exceeds it in "take." For the foreign traveler now arriving at
New York's Kennedy airport, the ride into Manhattan is still
eye-opening, but in a new way: litter and slums line the Van
Wyck Expressway through Jamaica, Queens, where rust and
graffiti festoon the old transit trains and bridges; the roads are
poor; there is no proper train into town—let alone something
as sleek and fast as in Hong Kong or Shanghai. Even baseball
players—as well as cars, toys, clothing, and electronics—are
produced better and cheaper abroad and are imported (in this
case, from the specialized industrial policy of the Dominican
Republic). Soccer—not baseball, football, or basketball—is by
far the world's foremost spectator sport and the sport that in-
volves the most kids; it is even gaining substantial market
share among young Americans, both boys and girls.

Hollywood no longer has an inherited, built-in meganarra-
tive—the presentation of life in modernity in all its weird and
quotidian forms: How women walk and speak, houses, murder,
seduction, sex, kitchens, raising children, "making it," excur-
sions, courtrooms, shopping centers, schools, hospitals, universities, and office buildings—the world, perhaps of your future.
The culture created by America and exported by its movies is
not gone; it's not even going. It has simply gone universal and
is now open to a vastly expanded range of contributors.

This is very likely to be a good thing for American and world culture, an opening to new ideas, talents, and energies. America's ambient culture is being enriched by foreign imports ranging from soccer to sushi, not to mention energetic Ph.D.'s in material and biological sciences. The big change is resulting from the successful absorption of American culture abroad to such an extent that it becomes not particularly American, but simply culture. The change is also powerfully propelled by the rise of new centers of self-awareness, confidence, identity, power, and, of course, money. The success of American culture in shaping the world has been enormous. And, like the English after Victoria, Americans are likely to find that it has made the world more comfortable for them long after their political and economic dominance has receded. Culture doesn't lead, it lags—both coming and going.

America is sure to remain a leader in cultural power, but there is a difference between being a cultural leader and an easy, almost un-self-conscious cultural dominance. Our research universities are the envy—and model—for the world. So too are our high-tech, biotech, and nanotech genre Silicon Valley–type firms, with their multinational, multiracial, and monocultural workforces of the bright, ambitious, educated, and driven. And there is also a powerful emergent American cultural force best represented by Barack and Michelle Obama: America might yet develop new meganarratives to succeed the world of modernity that will seize the world's hearts, fears, longings, and energies. But no matter how creative its creative people become, as in the realms of economic and political power, America is unlikely to remain the cultural hegemon, the overwhelmingly dominant source of cultural memes.

FOUR

Sovereign Wealth and Other Government Funds

By the mid-2000s, the first threat to the neoliberal dream appeared on the horizon. This was not, however, because governments were in revolt and becoming too activist. Rather, it was because certain governments were becoming too rich.

SOVEREIGN WEALTH FUNDS: WHEN GOVERNMENTS BECOME TOO RICH

Andrew Rozanov appears to have been the first writer to publicize the term *sovereign wealth fund,* back in 2005. Each part of the name had a meaning. The *funds* were just that—accumulations of assets invested worldwide. These were concerned with *wealth*; that is, their principal purpose was not industrial development, stabilization policy, support of the welfare state, or some other government function, but rather to park government wealth now for use in the future and meanwhile to obtain as high a return on investment as possible. The wealth had already been accumulated through either resource exports or trade surpluses. These funds were *sovereign* because their owners were not individuals who were subject to governments, but rather were governments themselves.

Since 2005, uses of the term have exploded: Google reports 3.2 million uses of the term *sovereign wealth funds* in 2008, compared with 435,000 in 2007, then 246,000 in 2006, and only 75,000 in 2005. The original coining of the term met a need— but the importance of that need has grown enormously since 2005.

Traditionally, governments that earned money were supposed to use it in defined ways. If they earned excess credits internally, governments were supposed to use them to pay down their national debts. If they earned funds externally— in forms and denominations that gave them claims on assets in other countries—they were either supposed to go to the other country's central bank or treasury and swap the funds for their own currency assets (or for gold, or for International Monetary Fund [IMF] "special drawing rights"). Or, more usually, governments would hold the funds as foreign-exchange reserves invested in the government debt of the country in which the wealth had been earned or the debt of major nations whose currency was widely used internationally (e.g., sterling or U.S. dollars). Anything else was considered a breach of international financial protocol: If a government were to invest in industry, the investments were supposed to be made in its own country, and not into some other government's economy. But government always reserves the right, and frequently exercises it, to make policies that might lower the value of some assets in its economy—a thing that is more difficult to do if some of the assets are owned by a sovereign. Government bonds of countries that play by the rules of the international financial game cause no trouble either in leaving the investing government vulnerable to some form of backdoor confiscation or in leaving the host government alarmed at implicit foreign interventions in its own economy.

The problem is that rates of return on government bonds of central countries in the global economy like the United States are low. They are the safe assets in the world economy. And if one rule of finance has held for the past 150 years, it is that safe assets are highly valued: There are, it seems, not enough places to park your wealth where it is not exposed to great risks, and so when investors find a safe asset—which almost always means a large-country government that they trust not to pursue a policy of out-and-out inflation—they are willing to pay very high prices for its assets. And high prices on average mean low average rates of return.

As accumulations piled up, these low rates of return began to seem unsatisfactory. Norway is presently generating enormous per capita wealth from its offshore hydrocarbons. The government and citizens of Norway don't want to spend their export earnings. Doing so would greatly push up the value of the kroner and destroy Norway's domestic industries—a pattern called the *Dutch disease*.

It was called the Dutch disease in memory of the economic difficulties the Netherlands experienced when in the 1960s, it did spend its earnings from offshore natural gas wells on imports into the domestic economy. The injection of new money pushed up the value of the Dutch guilder and severely hurt the competitive position of Dutch industry. It was a powerful lesson: If a country wants to keep its economy healthy, it can't just spend massive oil earnings; it must somehow hold those earnings offshore, in another currency, and tap into them slowly. Better to use the export earnings to buy imports not this year but rather a generation hence and in the meantime to save the earnings in a sovereign wealth fund.

Where, however, should you invest it? A fund invested in U.S. Treasury securities would be lucky to earn 2 percent above inflation: When you go to spend it twenty-five years down the road, you only have 25 percent more real purchasing power than you would have if you spent it today. In a world in which investments in stocks are expected to earn a real return of more than 8 percent per year on average, prudent investments made now should produce four times their current purchasing power if you are willing to let them ride for a generation. To sacrifice three-quarters of the wealth that Norwegians should have a generation hence from their postponement of consumption seemed a very high price to pay. And what would Norway buy by paying such a high price? Simply a reputation as a "good citizen" in international finance. That did not seem like such a good idea.

Hence, there came about Norway's sovereign wealth fund, one of the first and still one of the largest, with about $350 billion in assets. The earliest sovereign wealth fund that we have tracked and that fits the bill is the Kuwait Investment Authority, which dates back to 1953 and which is right now worth perhaps $200 billion. But there are also, right now, the Singapore Investment Corporation (perhaps $300 billion at present) and Singapore's Temasek Holdings ($200 billion?), the Korea

Investment Corporation, the Abu Dhabi Investment Authority ($600 billion?), the China Investment Corporation ($200 billion?), and the Stabilization Fund of the Russian Federation (with the recent drop in oil prices, its worth is suddenly down to perhaps $160 billion). Investments that are sovereign wealth funds and that agree to be called this held, in 2007, about $3.5 trillion—not a mere drop in the bucket in a world with perhaps $75 trillion of total property, much of which is in the form of people's houses. That a big hunk of that $3.5 trillion of mostly liquid assets is composed of investments by one government in the enterprises and property governed by another is definitely a fact of interest.

Probably more important in the long run is that sovereign wealth funds—and other government-controlled accumulations of foreign assets—are very likely to grow. There is an estimated $6 trillion of official foreign exchange reserves worldwide. That number is growing rapidly. The governments—mostly of countries that are still relatively not rich—that hold the bulk of those assets are unlikely to long remain happy holding them in liquid dollar- or euro-denominated government bonds. Doing so means annually sacrificing at least $400 billion of potential return relative to diversified market investments of the same degree of risk as the economy as a whole. And there is an additional $5 trillion in government-controlled pension funds, development funds, and state stakes in private enterprises. At the moment, sovereign governments may hold as much as a quarter of total global financial wealth.

The rapid growth of sovereign wealth funds has reinforced long-standing worries of foreign ownership and control of domestic enterprises. To be bossed around even indirectly by foreigners with money is not ideal. To be bossed around by foreign governments that need not have the transparent, money-grubbing objectives of bosses and shareholders worldwide but rather the potentially very different objectives of governments is more disturbing. President Gerald Ford established the interagency Committee on Foreign Investments in the United States (CFIUS) in 1975, in response to concerns about foreign investors in U.S. companies deemed to be important to national defense. The committee acquired some teeth and the possibility of a broader remit with the Exon-Florio Amendment to the Omnibus Trade and Competitiveness Act of 1998. Even Germany has begun to worry about foreign control of German companies and, in August 2008, began vetting foreign investments that lead to acquisition of a more than 25 percent stake in a German company on behalf of a non-European investor. The European Union is thinking increasingly about expanding dual-class shareholdership so that control remains in Europe even if ownership is more broadly diffused.

Where did these government wealth accumulations come from? There are three main streams: oil revenues, export surpluses, and "lemon socialist" funds.

NATURAL RESOURCES

The Kennedy-Johnson administration chose economic historian and development economist Walt Whitman Rostow to be national security adviser. This was the last time that economic development was thought, on the bureaucratic level, to be at least as important for the long-term national security of the United States as weapons systems. (It turned out badly: Rostow ended up to be more of a hawk on intervention in Vietnam than anybody else, save his brother Eugene V. Debs Rostow.) Rostow argued that the world economy went through long-term Kondratiev cycles of growth and development driven by Malthusian processes of resource exhaustion followed by Schumpeterian waves of innovation and exploration. A decade or two during which resource prices would rise higher and higher and growth would slow as industrialists economized on expensive natural resource inputs would be followed by a generation in which technological change or resource discovery would remove a bottleneck and create the opportunity for a decade or two of rapid growth. Kondratiev and Schumpeter thought that there was something in the water that made these waves occur with a regular periodicity of fifty years— twenty-five years of rising and then twenty-five years of falling natural resource prices. Rostow was cagier and would only say that the waves were "irregular."

In the recent world economy, resource prices reached a trough in 1986, after the world growth slowdown that started in the early 1970s had created slack demand and oversupply for many resources and, perhaps more important, after the Kingdom of Saudi Arabia made a decision in 1986 that its interest was in a relatively low price of oil. A low price for oil pleased the U.S. government, staved off major efforts at energy conservation and the development of alternative energy technologies, and starved the Islamic revolutionaries of the Party of Ali entrenched in Iran of funds to modernize their military and cause additional trouble in the Middle East. By the mid-2000s, the cycle had turned. Growing concern about global warming had created

the expectation that the open-carbon-cycle world-energy economy had only one more generation to go—in which case, the
interest of OPEC was not in maintaining the price of oil low
enough to attain political ends and to keep the North Atlantic
addicted to oil, but rather to maximizing the funds that could
be extracted over the next generation. The industrialization of
China and the appearance on the horizon of the industrialization of India made natural-resource owners all over the globe
look forward to very high relative demand for what they mined
and pumped. It thus greatly increased their reserve prices,
below which they simply would leave the stuff in the ground.
A huge chunk of this oil wealth was owned by governments—
and did not fit easily at all with the drive to neoliberal utopia.

THE EXPORT-LED MANUFACTURING ROAD

Oil-based sovereign wealth funds have proved to be less important and less anxiety creating—at least for the moment—
than the accumulated holdings of governments of export-based
manufacturing economies such as China, which itself holds
about $2.5 trillion in its various funds and reserves. Dani Rod-
rik argues that there is only one recipe for successful, rapid,
long-term industrial development, though there are three
ways that developing countries can generate jumps in economic activity:

1. By attracting "hot money" from rich countries with
    investors who are subject to fits of irrational
    exuberance

2. By exporting commodities whose prices are rising and by using those price rises to fuel expanded domestic consumption

3. By moving labor from low-productivity, near-subsistence agriculture into manufacturing by adapting and adopting the machine-based manufacturing technologies of the industrial revolution.

only one that works

The first two roads tend to produce short-term booms followed by crashes and reversals. Borrowing from overseas allows a country to feel rich and spend more for a while on domestic consumption and investment, but does not expand manufacturing and exports. Because the money funding the boom is hot and foreign investors are fickle, the flow eventually reverses itself. Moreover, the natural channels for money raised by borrowing from overseas are nontradables, like construction and elite luxury consumption. The second raises the requirements for imports in the long run, and the first does not expand exports. Thus, when the turn of the business cycle comes, the country will then find itself in a very bad bargaining position in world markets, and countries with weak positions end up with very poor terms of trade: The prices of exported commodities fall relative to imported industrial products. The long-term benefits of domestic economic growth will thus take the form of foreigners' ability to purchase one's exports cheaply, rather than one of sustained income growth and improvements in living standards at home. For these reasons, reliance on foreign capital is an unwise long-term strategy for economic growth (unless your domestic entrepreneurs are the equivalents of the Jay Goulds and the Leland Stanfords of nineteenth-century America, financiers who took the hot money of irrationally exuberant British investors and left them holding empty corporate shells as they tunneled the wealth into other, tightly held vehicles).

Relying on periods of primary product-led export booms to fuel growth is even worse in the long run. Commodity prices are the original boom-bust cycles. High commodity prices produce the "Dutch disease" in an economy—a period in which investment in manufacturing and other nonprimary export tradable-goods industries is crowded out. And the politics surrounding commodity booms very often turn ugly, as the political game becomes not how does the country collectively manage economic growth but rather how does a faction steal the resource wealth. Nigeria has been cursed by its oil wealth; Russia, too.

resource curse

The third road is the only one that has ever been successfully followed for generation-spanning fast growth. Ever since the initial industrial revolution in Britain, the countries that have grown most rapidly have been those that have found an industry or a set of industries into which they can move large amounts of labor out of low-productivity peasant agriculture. But in an economy overwhelmingly consisting of low-productivity, subsistence-income peasants, domestic demand for the output of any industry is always limited. Move large amounts of labor into any domestic industry, and the price at which you can sell its output quickly falls off because the other folks are just too poor to buy much. Rapid industrialization and growth is only likely to be attainable with large exports. And large exports require (1) a willingness to import on the part of other countries and (2) an exchange rate that keeps the value of the domestic currency low enough to make large-scale exports possible.

Such a low enough value of the domestic currency tends to lead to massive accumulations of foreign-exchange positions. Otherwise, demand and supply leads to upward pressure on domestic currency values. An appreciating currency leads to rising domestic costs relative to foreign costs in export industries and cuts short the process of export expansion that fuels industrialization and rapid growth. Thus, to maintain export-led growth, the government must intervene in markets and take steps to somehow keep domestic costs down relative to foreign costs.

One way to do so is through explicit industrial policy: Have the government subsidize the expansion of firms in the "modern" sector, trying to spur growth beyond domestic demand. The long-term hope is that successful growth will eventually expand the domestic middle class and its purchasing power enough so that in the end, the subsidy will no longer be needed—that domestic prices of modern goods will rise as the middle class grows. As William Easterly points out every day of the week (and twice on Mondays), this is an extraordinarily risky strategy. First, it is potentially wasteful. How will a weak and corrupt government—and governments in poor countries are almost inevitably weak and corrupt—be able to channel its subsidies to just those firms whose lack of profits arises from production having temporarily raced ahead of the growth of demand? Those are the firms that will be healthy in the long run. Opposed to them are the firms that are simply inefficient.

A government is not well equipped to discern which is which. In the end, the subsidies will likely be allocated by a different principle: They will go to firms that are run by the nephew of the vice minister of finance.

Thus, says Easterly, the likelihood that a country that adopts an aggressive policy of subsidizing domestic industry will experience a long-term growth boom "would seem to be pretty low." The historical record consists not just of some East Asian countries that succeeded in industrial policy but also of many others that failed.

> African and Latin American [economies] . . . tried industrial policies over the past six decades with low and erratic growth as a result. . . . [F]orcing investments into industrialization led to a huge pileup of debt in Latin America in the 1970s . . . a debt crisis in 1982 . . . subsequent lost decades . . . the Ajaokuta steel mill in Nigeria which went through $6 billion but never produced a bar of steel, . . . Tanzanian manufacturing, which had negative growth of output per worker despite heavy capital investments.

A better, more automatic, less manipulable, and less easily distorted by corruption and rent-seeking way to accomplish the same end is for the government to concentrate on keeping the value of the currency low. Exchange-rate manipulation is a way of creating a broad-based subsidy program that is not easily subject to the what-do-you-do-when-your-nephew-comes-calling? problem. Tapping global export markets allows expansion of high-productivity modern manufacturing without running into the limits that would otherwise be imposed by inadequate demand for modern goods from a weak and poor domestic middle class. And in the long run in a globalized world, domestic prices must converge with global prices. Investments in industries that can successfully export at global prices are investments in industries that will be profitable and sustainable even in the long run as the configuration of domestic prices approaches world values.

Thus, it may not be too much to say that the best possible or at least the best attainable of industrial policies for sustained development is an undervalued exchange rate. The developmental states that use currency-value manipulation to send their industrial sectors the message to transfer labor from near-subsistence agriculture to the industrial production of modern goods are the most successful.

China, of course, has been the most extreme and the most successful example of this development strategy in recent years—in fact, it is the most successful example of large-scale economic development ever. Its growth has been the result of extraordinarily rapid, large-scale structural transformation—from farm to city, from western interior to eastern coast, from agriculture to manufacturing production—fueled by extraordinarily large exports to the United States and Europe. The U.S. willingness to serve as importer of last resort was an essential block of China's development strategy, based as it was on rapidly expanding production in "modern" goods.

China, however, was far from alone. Alongside and before China came the other economies of East and Southeast Asia. And before them came the countries of Western Europe via the post–World War II Bretton Woods system of fixed exchange rates. And before them came the United States, whose pre–World War I manufacturing export growth was fueled by both protective tariffs surrounding domestic industry and a low currency value caused by the fear that William Jennings Bryan and company might actually win an election and abandon the gold standard to fulfill their campaign plank of making interest rates low and farm gate prices high via the free coinage of silver at a ratio of sixteen to one.

PILING UP SURPLUSES

A policy of an undervalued currency does not, however, maintain itself. A country, especially a rapidly growing one, must impose financial controls to restrict imports of "hot money." Foreigners seeking to invest and benefit must be required to import capital goods and build factories directly with their money, lest they put upward pressure on the value of the currency. And as exports grow, the foreign-exchange earnings of exporters grow as well. These earnings will then show up on the demand side of the foreign-exchange market, raising the value of the currency, as exporters try to turn the earnings into useful domestic cash. Rising demand raises prices—in this case, the value of the domestic currency.

The government must step in to offset the rise in demand for domestic currency by increasing the supply. It must print and sell the domestic currency and, in the process, buy up the foreign exchange and hold it. A policy of export-led industrialization via an undervalued currency is also a policy of massive accumulation of foreign exchange by the government.

For a while, this accumulation of foreign exchange does not pose a problem. Countries and their central banks like to hold dollar-denominated assets as part or all of their foreign-exchange reserve portfolios. The devastating financial crises of 1994–1995 in Mexico and 1997–1998 in East Asia impressed governments everywhere with the lesson that international financial markets are dangerous places, and that it is wise for a country to have much more in the way of hard-currency foreign-exchange reserves than had previously been thought. So for a while, governments are content to allow the government-owned tranche of the difference between their booming exports and their imports to accumulate as a balance in dollar-denominated U.S. Treasury securities parked inside the Federal Reserve Bank of New York.

Such accumulation cannot go on forever. First, accounts held in U.S. Treasuries pay low interest rates, and while this does not matter as long as the account balances are small, it matters a lot for poor countries, especially when dollar balances are large. The larger the government holdings, the greater the pressure to seek and find higher-yielding investment vehicles. Second, global imbalances will come to an end someday. When they come to an end, that end is likely to take the form of some burst of devaluation or inflation inside the United States. Thus, at the end of the day, it is better if the government accumulations from export surpluses are held in real rather than nominal assets: held in forms that will hold all or much of their value rather than lose it in an inflation or devaluation of the U.S. dollar.

THE ONCE AND FUTURE DOLLAR

And what of the dollar? Could a sudden, sharp decline in the value of the dollar destroy foreign government wealth holdings and make them a curiosity and not a problem? (Back in 1985, remember, the fear was that Japan was going to own America and then Japan's accumulated and capitalized export surpluses largely vanished between the Plaza Hotel and the Louvre as the dollar fell in value.) Alternatively, can foreign debts owed by America lead to a dollar crash that cripples the U.S. economy in a manner analogous to the Mexican crisis of 1994–1995, the East Asian crisis of 1997–1998, or the Argentine crisis of 2001– 2003—only marvelously bigger? It is likely that the answers to these questions are no and no.

For at least an entire decade, economists have been antici- pating a relatively sharp fall in the dollar down to balanced- trade fundamentals. Yet, rich private foreigners value having large chunks of their money in the United States as a form of political risk insurance. They are continuing to increase the size of that chunk they wish to hold in America. Foreign govern- ments continue to increase their holdings of dollar-denominated securities to make sure that they can keep exporting to the United States at a pace that allows for export-led growth and thus produces domestic social peace. And the role of the dollar as the key currency of the international monetary system creates a large demand to hold dollars as reserve stores of wealth—the "exorbitant privilege" of which Charles de Gaulle complained two generations ago. As long as these three factors keep operating, the value of the dollar will remain relatively high. And these three factors have already shown remarkable persistence. Their end is likely to be far off, and unlikely to be sudden.

Moreover, the fact that the United States has borrowed and its debt is denominated in its own currency, dollars, while Mexico, East Asia, and Argentina borrowed in a foreign currency, also dollars, makes a world of difference. Huge debt owed in foreign currency is severely disciplined, and you have to painfully earn the currency. Huge debt in your own currency—in dollars—is different; the United States can always create more dollars, and its value is everyone's problem.

The maintenance of the dollar at a value stable enough so that its changes do not disrupt the finances of dollar-holding foreign governments is now a common aim of world governments. If they can keep the dollar from losing value rapidly, they will do so. Other countries lose a fortune when the dollar falls: Their holdings of dollar-denominated securities are now worth much less in the coin that has meaning to them. As the value of the dollar falls, it makes room for the dollar prices at which the United States sells its exports to rise, while the dollar debts America owes stay the same. Consequently, the U.S. foreign debt becomes less and not more burdensome as the dollar falls in value. It means, as Nixon's Treasury Secretary John Connally—a man whom his deputy Paul Volcker said was strongly in favor of taking bold action but did not care much which particular action he took as long as it was bold—quipped to his foreign counterparts that instability in the dollar is "our currency, but your problem."

A sharp fall in the dollar does mean that the processes we examine in this book are considerably accelerated. When the dollar is worth less, Americans, because they hold dollars, are poorer and foreigners richer. The pace at which America loses its various forms of soft-power influence accelerates. And the speed at which pieces of America are bought up by others is more rapid the lower the value of the dollar, because a 50 percent lower value of the dollar is essentially a half-off asset sale. The resources of foreigners continue to grow at their previous rate, but foreigners will get much more bang for their euros when the investors move their money into the United States when the dollar is low.

In fact, as long as the dollar remains the centerpiece of the world economy, there is a strong sense that successful global economic growth requires an increase in U.S. indebtedness to the rest of the world—and that the U.S. international debt is not a problem at all, but rather, as Alexander Hamilton would have said were he alive today in his old corner office at the Treasury Department, a global blessing. Just as a growing demand for cash produced by a rush to safety in financial panics requires a central bank to act as lender of last resort to head off universal bankruptcy, so a growing demand for dollars by foreign governments and investors to expand world trade requires that the United States act as importer of last resort—and let its trade deficit rise (and its export and import-competing manufacturing sector shrink)—to create that global liquidity.

Back under the Bretton Woods system, Western European countries that accumulated export surpluses sought to preserve the surpluses' real value against eventual dollar depreciation by parking their assets in gold. These countries sought to use the loophole that the U.S. government had never abandoned the gold standard but only suspended convertibility to transform dollar export surpluses into gold asset holdings. It did not work. Now the Chinese and other export-surplus reserve-accumulation countries are making noises about how the IMF should midwife the transformation of their dollar-denominated holdings into a form that will not lose value if the dollar does. This hope was not successful a generation ago and will not be successful now. The only effective long-term way to guard the value of reserve accumulations is to invest them in real and not nominal property—that is, to turn the foreign-exchange holdings of governments into the actively invested assets of sovereign wealth funds.

SOVEREIGN WEALTH FUNDS AND THE CURRENT CRISIS

The financial crisis beginning in 2007 has had a mixed impact on sovereign wealth funds. Values of these funds have fallen as general asset values have fallen—from perhaps $3.5 trillion to $2 trillion and change. But the share of total global wealth held in sovereign wealth funds has not fallen. And the huge accumulations held in U.S. Treasury securities have not fallen, but rather have risen in value. When the funds are transferred—as they will be—into higher-yielding asset classes less vulnerable to dollar depreciation or domestic U.S. inflation, the funds will purchase more and not less real economic ownership.

Moreover, total equity ownership by governments has been further swelled by the financial crisis and the accompanying deep recession, as a third category of publicly owned money has been added to the pool. The first wave of sovereign wealth funds was the accumulated oil revenues of countries from Norway to Saudi Arabia. The second wave was the accumulated foreign-exchange reserves of rapidly industrializing Asian powers that felt that lowballing their currency values via manipulating the exchange rate was the road to rapid structural transformation. The third wave is being triggered by the financial crisis. It is a wave of "lemon socialism": As a result of the crisis, governments around the world are taking enormous stakes and positions in financial and operating companies. These stakes and positions will not easily be unwound. And until they are unwound, all of the issues surrounding the first two waves of sovereign wealth funds involve this wave as well—and when the dust settles, this wave is likely to be very big.

The drivers of the growing importance of sovereign wealth funds are now four, and none of them is at risk from the current recession:

1. The need, as governmental holdings grow larger and larger, for higher rates of return on them and insurance against devaluation and inflation
2. Global imbalances that are inevitable as industrializing countries grasp for export markets and put downward pressure on their currency values to do so

3. Oil accumulations
4. Government-run pension and related funds, government reserves, and government-controlled financial and industrial companies.

THE NEOLIBERAL PROGRAM
FOR SOVEREIGN WEALTH FUNDS

Government ownership of industry and finance—even government minority silent-partnership stakes—sat very uneasily with the program of the neoliberals' dream. The market's calculation of social costs and benefits presumed that everybody was self-interested—was pursuing their own profit and nothing else. Only thus could the theory of the market economy guarantee that ambition would counteract ambition, that the alchemy of the invisible hand would transform private vices into public benefits, and that resources would flow to their best and most profitable uses. Free trade by market-oriented and wealth-seeking individuals was, the tradition stemming from Adam Smith had long argued, best for all. Under the standard assumptions—no increasing returns to scale, well-defined property rights, the absence of positive and negative externalities, the absence of market power, no significant information asymmetries about what was really being bought and sold—free-market acts of exchange between consenting adults would create a world in which all possible win-win trades, and only those trades, were carried out. The resulting distribution of income would be unequal, but it would not be unfair—or, rather, it would only be unfair to the extent that the initial distribution of property and other valuable resources was unfair. The market system would not amplify and might well diminish already existing unfairness as high prices for scarce commodities induced people to invent their way around them and thus reduced the value of scarce properties.

But the belief that the market was best for all in this sense did not mean that it was best for each, or best if some of its rigorous conditions were not met. If you had market power or privileged information, you could make yourself better off by using it. And if you could organize your fellows who owned the same kind of property as you did into a cartel . . . The logic of the market depended on making people follow the rules of the game. Hence antitrust policy.

Adherence to the rules of the neoliberal game became even more important when you looked beyond the Adam Smithian assumptions for a more realistic take. In the real world, scale and especially technological knowledge were key causes of wealth—and the acquisition of your technological knowledge by others might well diminish your terms of trade and standard of living. Recall that at least half of American economic growth comes from technological and organizational progress in the form of innovation. These gains from better knowledge of technology and organization are not all seized by those who pioneer the innovations that turn out to be most useful, but rather spill over into the broader economy usually quite nearby.

It is here that sovereign wealth funds may threaten to become a serpent in the garden. Governments would pursue objectives—for technology transfer, for strategic political advantage, for the redistribution of rents, for the differential acquisition of markets—that would lead them to different decisions than would have been made by profit-oriented market agents. Was a host country government supposed to stand by and allow its economy to be warped in the interests of some other government? But could a host country government afford to exclude whole categories of world wealth accumulation from being used to build buildings, factories, and infrastructure within its borders? If there were to be sovereign wealth funds—which there were—and if they were to be consistent with the stable, onward march toward the neoliberal utopia, there needed to be explicit rules of the game to govern them and to make it clear how they were "allowed" and not "allowed" to deviate from the narrow logic of the market. Moreover, it was imperative that what the funds did do would promptly be made transparent.

Edwin Truman, of the Peterson Institute for International Economics and former assistant secretary of the Treasury, has valiantly spearheaded the effort to bring sovereign wealth funds under the neoliberal umbrella. The problem from the U.S. perspective was, first, a redistribution of relative wealth from America to the rest of the world; second, a redistribution of relative wealth to governments and citizens of countries that were not seen as safe and that "historically have not been major players in international finance and have had little or no role in shaping the practices, norms, and conventions governing the international financial system"; and, third, a redistribution to governments that were not predictable market actors seeking highest risk-adjusted market return but rather had other, more complicated objectives in mind.

From Truman's perspective, the right solution to these government-owned wealth accumulations was for them to exercise
"due influence" but not "undue influence" in the companies
that they invested in. It was impossible to lay down a rule that
governments should invest only in Treasury securities—the
gap between Treasury and private-sector yields made such a
rule unacceptable to those who, after all, had the money. It
was similarly unthinkable to limit government investments to
passive, nonvoting, second-class common or preferred stock
investments or to bonds—to grant them "ownership" but no
voice in control. Ownership without control leads to loss by
theft, as those with control figure out some way to tunnel the
valuable assets out into some other privately held vehicle, leaving those who held the shares but did not sit on the board or
choose the executives with nothing but an empty, overly indebted shell. So foreign governments must hold high-yielding
bond and equity stakes in corporations whose operations are
located in other countries, and they must exercise due control
over management. Nevertheless, governments must also be
constrained to, as Truman puts it, "reduce the probability that
the government owners of sovereign wealth funds . . . seek to
exercise 'undue influence' over the decisions of financial institutions in which they have significant stakes."

This is a task for supervisors and regulators, of whom it is
"reasonable to ask . . . what procedures they have in place" to
ensure that the non-market-actor owners act like normal profit-
seeking investors. This does "complicate the enforcement of
U.S. securities laws. But this is a fact of life. . . . The challenge . . . is how to make the world safer for sovereign wealth

funds and maintain our own, open market–based regime in which private-sector actors are the major players."

Truman explains how to address this challenge:

> Agree upon a set of best practices, or a standard, for sovereign wealth funds to make them more account-able. . . . Transparency has a large part to play in estab-lishing such accountability, but it is only part of the game. Based upon the 'scoreboard' for 33 sovereign wealth funds that I have developed, I am confident that the union of the actual practices of those funds provides an appropriate framework for a set of best practices.

Why is he confident? He believes that the goal is not unat-tainable: "At least one sovereign wealth fund currently, volun-tarily complies with each of the 25 elements in the scoreboard." And his lobbying campaign has, in our view, already been much more successful than we would have anticipated.

Nevertheless, we are much less optimistic that these large, government-owned wealth accumulations can be so curbed.

FIVE

Where Did All Their
Money Come From?

How did all those dollars pile up out there? Are they, somehow, related to the U.S. financial and economic crisis? The first explanatory thread pulls out of the spaghetti bowl quickly and easily: We Americans spent more than we earned; we consumed more than we produced. We borrowed the money to buy the stuff from the people who produced it abroad and sold it to us. We paid them in dollars; they took the dollars and lent them back to us, so we could do it again. It worked well all around. They sold more, banked the money, and felt richer; we bought more and felt prosperous.

Year after year, the United States imported more goods and services than it exported. In 2006, the gap reached $750 billion, almost $6,500 per U.S. household, some 6 percent of GDP. And that was only one year; America ran a similar tab in 2005, and not hugely less in 2004.

Some of this deficit was useful and appropriate. Go back more than sixty years, to the first years after World War II, to the beginning of the great global boom from 1945 to 1973, which was then the best generation ever seen for world economic growth. (Whether we are now in the middle of an even better generation—whether 1995–2020 will prove to be better—is right now in our hands.) Just after World War II, the rebuilding economies of Western Europe and Japan believed that their governments had to hold enough financial reserves in order to grease the flow of imports and exports, and they did not trust each other to maintain their currency values. All governments worldwide insisted on holding dollars in reserve in their treasuries and central banks. If, they thought, they did not have enough dollars to ride out a financial crisis, then they needed to raise interest rates and discourage imports until their surplus of exports over imports had earned them enough credits. They could then buy the dollar-denominated securities that they wanted to hold in reserve. And they did so.

But there was an arithmetic problem. By raising its interest rates and raising its level of unemployment, one country can diminish its imports and create an export surplus to earn the foreign exchange needed to buy dollar-denominated securities to top off its reserves. But what happens if all countries try to do so? Until we earth citizens begin large-scale, interstellar trade with the planet Vulcan, global trade must balance. Some big country—in the event, the United States—must run a big deficit. The sum of the export surplus of all other countries must equal the trade deficit of the United States. And if the U.S. Treasury and Federal Reserve are unwilling to craft macroeconomic policies to allow the U.S. trade deficit to rise when other countries have a hunger for dollar-denominated reserves, then all that the other countries will do by trying to build up their reserves is to, collectively, beggar themselves.

Back in the 1950s, the "dollar shortage" as a potential and an actual source of drag, sluggish growth, and deflation was owned by economist Robert Triffin. In the end, the United States was willing to play the roles of system maintainer and importer of last resort.

Over the past generation, something very similar has been occurring. Foreign governments and investors, mostly in Asia, have believed that macroeconomic policy and portfolio equilibrium require that they boost their holdings of dollar-denominated financial assets to levels that two decades ago would have been regarded as absurd and unbelievable.

THE ARITHMETIC OF THE U.S. DEFICIT

In every year since 1976, the United States has run international trade deficits that collectively add up to over $7 trillion. More than 70 percent of that $7 trillion has been added since 2000. Yet, curiously enough, surveys report that Americans owe only about $3.5 trillion more to foreigners than foreigners owe to Americans. Where did the other $3.5 trillion go? Economists dispute: Some think it likely that foreigners' earnings from their American properties that are then reinvested in the United States are massively undercounted, while other analysts think it more likely that foreigners have obtained very low rates of return on investments in the United States—either because the foreign investors are inept, because their American counterparts are not too scrupulous, or because they have been sacrificing return for safety. Perhaps the net debt is currently only $3.5 trillion. That comes to over $30,000 per U.S. household, and it will grow. And perhaps it is already significantly larger.

In addition to the $3.5 trillion net that Americans owe foreigners, there are additional cross-holdings that amount to perhaps $6 trillion each: $6 trillion of foreign property owned by Americans and $6 trillion of American property owned by foreigners. Tracing it out quickly becomes tangled and nearly impossible: American individuals with portfolio investments in foreign countries, American-owned companies with subsidiaries overseas, foreigners who have made portfolio investments in American companies with foreign subsidiaries that have in turn built plant and equipment back in the United States. There are powerful reasons to invest across borders in this second (or is it third?) age of globalization, two of which are (1) that investing across borders is a way for companies to acquire better access to foreign markets and better control over their domestic market's foreign suppliers of goods, and (2) that it is a cheap way of ensuring against poor performance at home via diversification.

WHY GLOBAL IMBALANCES?

Standard economics textbooks say that when the dollar—or any other currency—piles up abroad as a result of a trade imbalance, its price will decline: Supply and demand will kick in to adjust exchange rates, which will adjust trade and money flows. Market forces will push up the Chinese renminbi against the dollar, raising the price of Chinese goods for American buyers and lowering the price of American goods for Chinese buyers while also making American goods more attractive, compared with imports, for American buyers. The United States will import less, produce more, and export more; China will export less. Balance will be restored. Clearly, this is not what happened.

Why? The renminbi-dollar exchange rate was not set and adjusted by markets the way the euro-dollar or Canadian-U.S. rates are. China pegged its exchange rate to the dollar and controlled any adjustments. How? If speculators sold renminbi for dollars and pushed down the value of the renminbi, China would simply buy up the renminbi, dipping into its vast store of dollars; in this way, China would protect itself from something like the disastrous 1997 Asian currency crisis. If speculators began to buy the renminbi with their dollars and pulled up its price, China would sell renminbi for dollars and add them to its pile. Markets could neither push the renminbi down nor push it up. The Chinese government could hold the renminbi-dollar exchange rate right where it wanted. In addition, the Chinese government maintained tight controls on its currency. International speculators and businesses—and Chinese ones, too—could not simply rush renminbi into or out of China. Chinese companies were not permitted to sell debt and stocks to foreigners, or buy foreign ones, without government approval.

Is it crazy, selling goods for paper dollars and just holding those dollars and buying nothing of tangible value with them?

A poor country like China subsidizing rich Americans? Yes, it is crazy.

But it is not completely crazy. Over the years, China has followed the example of other previous fast-developing Asian manufacturing countries, but on an enormously larger scale. It, too, has been pulling itself up by its bootstraps through export-led development. China jump-started its acceleration by attracting foreign companies to set up in China and produce for foreign markets: Some two-thirds of Chinese exports today still come from companies with direct investment by foreign firms. These companies bringing technology and know-how to China have been the engine of Chinese development—at first simple and very cheap labor to sew garments, cobble shoes, and assemble imported components for electronic devices. And as capabilities in China increase, a larger proportion of the value of those products will be made in China by Chinese workers and subcontractors. China still has a very long way to climb the value-added ladder. Guesstimates place Chinese value added for their exports at under one-third, up from one-fifth five years ago. To a very considerable extent, China's exports still consist of Chinese workers assembling imported components. So when we say, "The United States imports from China," we are really saying, "The United States imports from China the outputs of an integrated trans-Asian production network with key nodes for the high end components in Japan, Taiwan, Singapore, and, for the brutish inputs, Australia."

This economic-development model has been an indisputable success, the fastest, biggest economic success in world history. China has grown by something close to 10 percent per year for over twenty years. That compounds to an eightfold increase in China's GDP. Exports generated higher-value jobs for poor peasants who poured off the farms, where the value of their work was extremely low, into higher-value-added employment in the mushrooming manufacturing cities. The foreign-dominated export sector served China not only as a job and income creator, but also as a kind of industrial craft school, and while education is expensive, it is usually worthwhile.

In Chapter 1, we noted that even in the United States—which lies at the forefront of the world economy, where technological and organizational progress is slowest because you cannot look, copy, and adapt but must instead invent from scratch—technological and organizational progress together account for half of GDP and two-thirds of labor productivity growth. The preponderance of growth generated by innovation is not captured by the initial innovator but spreads through imitation into the local economy.

Most economic growth does not come from adding to visible productive resources—the number of hands and machines, and the skills that formal education has given those hands—but from working smarter. If you sell the results of your workers' hands and your machines for less than they cost, but in the process acquire the knowledge needed to work smarter, you come out ahead. And imitation and practice are the best ways to do so. An enormous share of China's economic growth is an unrecompensed by-product of what businesses do as technological and organizational knowledge that spills over into the local industrial ecosystem. And increasing the speed of that process by undervaluing the renminbi and so keeping the export engine humming and growing has been a very good long-run deal for China. It also offered a good deal to the United States, to the extent that it means that Americans get lots of good stuff cheap. What's more, Americans also get the opportunity to redeploy their labor and capital into activities that create higher value—labor and capital that would otherwise be making import-competing products. This is the opportunity; it can be squandered, and it was.

What did China do with all those dollars? It kept them. Some were diversified into Japanese yen and euros, but most—estimates place it at about 70 percent, although there are no reliable official accounts available—stayed in dollars. They were parked in the safest, most liquid place to park excess money which was also the only available parking place for money at that scale: China recycled the dollars back into the U.S. financial system. Where else could you put megapacks of dollars? Some went directly into the banks, a good amount went into what are called *agencies*—the debts of Freddie Mac and Fannie May, the giant "government-sponsored" mortgage lenders. Most went directly into Treasuries, financing ballooning government deficits resulting from the Iraq war and the tax cuts, and keeping interest rates down, freeing other money to circulate within the financial system, and allowing American corporations to borrow money to buy back their stock and American homeowners to use their houses as gigantic ATMs from which they extracted the equity to keep spending.

Could China have avoided getting into its present situation of holding dollars? Yes, but if, and only if, it had decided to back away from the manufacturing export-intensive development strategy. The Chinese save a stupendous amount of their incomes, over 40 percent. Some of this savings is cycled by the Chinese financial system into new investment—most of which goes to expanding production, and that production has to be bought by someone; the rest piles up, unspent. If the Chinese themselves don't buy what they produce, then foreigners must, or else everything stops. Foreigners did, and everything barreled ahead.

THE MACHINE MUST STOP—SOMEDAY

Could this export-driven growth machine continue? Many economists feared that it could not and that everything would end badly. For an entire decade, economists have been anticipating a relatively sharp fall in the dollar. At the dollar's current value against a basket of international currencies—or even at a value of the dollar some 30 percent lower than its current value—demand by others for U.S. exports will be lower than demand by Americans for imports from abroad. Moreover, foreigners now own more property in the United States than Americans own abroad. Because the interest and dividends on this extra property will eventually be spent where the foreigners live, we would ultimately expect the dollar to decline to a value at which the United States generates an export surplus large enough to match that flow of U.S. income out to our foreign creditors.

Five years ago, most economists bet that the era of the high dollar would soon come to an end and that its sudden end was the greatest macroeconomic danger facing the world economy—much greater than the danger of runaway over-speculation in mortgage-backed securities and real estate prices.

Over the past five years, however, expectations have shifted. The fact that the financial crisis of 2007–? has not materially diminished the value of the dollar has made people think again. The crisis was made in the desert between Los Angeles and Las Vegas, and if an American crisis that increases American risks does not reduce the value of the American dollar, what would? It is the old adage that we've come back to several times in this book: When you owe the bank thousands, you have a problem, but when you owe the bank billions, the bank has a problem. A collapse in the value of the dollar may still come. But it's no sure thing. The maintenance of the dollar at a value stable enough so that its changes do not disrupt the finances of dollar-holding foreign governments is now a common aim of the governments that matter. If they can keep the dollar from losing value rapidly, they will do so.

The blunt fact is that a dollar collapse means that other countries lose a fortune—their holdings of dollar-denominated securities would be worth much less in their own currency. And despite much talk and anxiousness, there is still no other currency, national or synthetic, that is ready and willing to substitute for the dollar, at scale, in this critical and demanding role.

Suppose that we are wrong. Suppose that there is a dollar crash sometime in the next five years. What then? It would be a signal for panic only if America owed other people the money in a currency it did not control—that is, renminbi or euros. If and when the U.S. government begins to borrow in renminbi or euros, start worrying. Until then, don't. A drop in the value of the dollar, even a big drop, is not the end of the American economy.

The key difference between the current episode, in which the United States owes very large debts relative to the size of the economy to foreign citizens and governments, and earlier debt episodes is that this time, the United States counts the money. The U.S. foreign debt is either in the form of titles to some form of real property—land, buildings, equities, or corporations—or in the form of debt denominated in dollars.

In 1997 and 1998, forward-looking investors sold assets denominated in baht, rupiah, won, and ringgit, and bought assets denominated in dollars. These asset sales themselves sharply pushed down the values of the baht, rupiah, won, and ringgit in terms of dollars. And all of a sudden, what had been a small problem for a "froth" of speculative companies riding the East Asian boom became an economy-wide catastrophe. Utilities, banks, and conglomerates, which carried large dollar-denominated debts but which were perfectly solvent and profitable when 900 won equaled one dollar, were completely and totally bankrupt when it took 1,500 won to equal one dollar. The collapse of the value of the won in early 1998 meant that every Korean conglomerate and bank suddenly owed twice as much in terms of its own Korea-located assets to its American creditors, and the Koreans simply could not pay. Something very similar hit Thailand, Indonesia, and Malaysia and even rattled Taiwan; China, whose currency was not freely tradable and whose markets were not open, withstood the onslaught.

Had the won stayed at 900 to the dollar, there would have been no financial crisis in Korea in 1998 and no recession in Korea in 1998–1999. There would have been a minor embarrassment and a few isolated bankruptcies of speculative ventures.

But fear of a crisis that would produce large-scale bankruptcies and recession triggered a fall in the won, which produced a crisis with large-scale bankruptcies and a sharp and steep recession: a vicious circle, in which fear creates the events that were feared, which there would have been no reason to fear, had people not been afraid of them. It is not quite "the only thing we have to fear is fear itself," for it is fear that sets in motion forces that produce nationwide chains of bankruptcies and defaults, shuttered factories, high unemployment, and falling production—and it is those things that are to be really feared for their own sake. But it is close.

It is important to recognize that large-scale currency mismatch—debts in a foreign currency, say dollars, and assets and revenues in the national currency—is a precondition for foreign debt to cause a major crisis like those of Argentina in 2001, East Asia in 1997–1998, Mexico in 1994–1995, Latin America in 1979–1985, or Sweden in 1992–1993. Analogies between the position of the United States as debtor economy now and these other, earlier debtor economies that proved so vulnerable to financial crisis are faulty. The difference is that the international debt of the United States today is denominated not in baht, ringgit, rupiah, or won or even in renminbi, yen, pounds, gold, or euros, but in dollars. There is now no currency mismatch.

The Asian surplus of saving over investment, production over spending, has on its other side an American deficit of savings relative to investment, production relative to spending. This deficit did not come about because investment grew; it came about because Americans essentially stopped saving. Government, businesses, and households spent everything they earned and then borrowed more, ultimately from the Chinese producers, in order to buy more. If you spend more than you produce, you have to import the extra product and borrow the money to pay for it.

What drove the American side of this tight, though uncomfortable, economic relationship?

Something very big changed in America between the post–World War II generation and the present time: That particular something was the distribution of the money generated by the growth of the American economy. In the first postwar generation, 1947 to 1973, American labor productivity—average output per hour worked—doubled (growing at a rate of about 2.5 percent per year). Median income—the income of the average American, the American sitting on the fifty-yard line, with half of Americans earning more and half less—rose at the same rate; it too doubled. As a society, America marched into prosperity in unwavering ranks, everyone advancing at the same rate. And Americans also managed to save about 7 percent of GDP each year.

Over the next thirty-plus years, from 1973 to 2005, productivity grew at a somewhat slower rate. Nevertheless, the awful decades of the 1970s and 1980s were offset by strong growth in the high-tech boom years of the 1990s, and overall labor productivity still increased by two-thirds or so. But the American middle class got almost nothing of that gain. The incomes of those smack in the middle of the American income distribution increased by only 14 percent over thirty years, and almost all of that gain had come in the late Clinton years of 1995–2000. Simultaneously, American savings (incomes minus spending) dried up completely: a phenomenon not seen since the Depression.

While the median American male's income stayed flat from 1973 to 2005, the gain went to the top 10 percent, and most of that went to the topmost reaches of the top 10 percent. The ratio of the top 1 percent to the middle fifth went from 10 to 26 times. What caused the change? A set of forces that include:

1. *An unprecedented rise in asset values:* The Dow Jones Industrial Average rose at about 1.3 percent per year between 1960 and 1980 (and that is not adjusted for inflation). Over the next twenty years, 1980 to 2000, it rose tenfold—1,000 percent. Whatever we may hear about America being a nation of shareholders, shareholdings are radically skewed toward the top: The top 10 percent owns 77 percent of all stocks. And the holdings are steeply skewed within the top 10 percent: The top 1 percent of American households owns one-third of all stocks, the next 9 percent owns 43 percent, and the remaining 90 percent of Americans owns 23 percent (including 401[k]s). Housing prices also rose, and the wealthiest families own the biggest houses and benefit disproportionally from the advantageous tax treatment lavished on home ownership.

2. *Government policy:* Under Eisenhower, whom no one ever called a radical, top tax brackets extended up to 90 percent (snaring marginal bracket dollars from no more than about three hundred very rich people); in the 1960s, they were about 70 percent; in 1986, they

were lowered to 28 percent and have moved around since, but were never pushed back up to the ranges that prevailed during the faster-growth, more equitable America of the first postwar period. They are now about 35 percent. Under George W. Bush, the government cut away at inheritance taxes (and even eliminated them entirely as of 2010, but only until January 1, 2011, when pre-Bush rates are scheduled to return unless the law is changed: The elderly rich are likely to be especially fearful around Christmas 2010). Inheritance taxes affect only the top 1.5 percent.

3. *Immigration:* Huge, recent waves of unskilled immigrants, legal and illegal, compete for low-wage jobs, pulling down the bottom of the income scale.

4. *Imports and offshoring:* The influx of imported goods pushed down employment and pricing power at American manufacturers, which typically paid higher wages than did the big-battalion service employers, retail and fast-food restaurants, squeezing wages. Moving industrial production offshore—even the threat to do so—holds down demands for higher wages. Offshoring, until recently confined to industrial production, is rapidly extending into white-collar jobs in such diverse industries as finance, insurance, accounting, law, and engineering—the product flows instantly through the Internet, enabling employment to relocate to places such as India and the Philippines, where comparable skills can cost as little as one-fifth of American rates.

5. *Decline of unions:* Unions more or less disappeared as a major force in most of the private sector. The Reagan administration was far more successful in its war on unions than in its war on drugs, beginning with the air-traffic-controller strike. And of course, increased foreign competition and the weakening of the giant, mass-production, oligopoly industries such as steel (the core of union power) combined to radically reduce unions' ability to sustain wages.

6. *Technology:* It is not the production of high-tech goods, but their use in business that is often cited as an important factor that has increased inequality. Whatever the findings of econometric analyses, it is difficult to argue that the U.S. economy uses more technology than, for example, Scandinavia or Germany, where significant increases in income inequality have not been recorded.

7. *Culture:* It seems to us that there has been a cumulating and massive cultural change regarding income inequality: CEO pay is a good indicator. In the 1960s, CEOs of large companies were on top of the income pile, paid as much as thirty times the average worker; by 2000, the ratio had gone up tenfold, to three hundred times the income of the average worker. It would be difficult to argue that CEOs, or their companies, performed better in the twenty-first century—when Congress voted to repeal the inheritance tax—than they did in the postwar period. Furthermore, this increase has been exceptionally high

in the United States relative to other OECD countries. American CEOs are paid about three times as much as their counterparts abroad. Only in Switzerland did CEOs' pay reach even 50 percent of their American counterparts.

We don't weigh these seven factors for their relative importance.

Is there a connection between rapidly rising inequality, stagnant middle-class earnings, and the collapse of savings in the United States? It is very likely that these trends are all closely linked. Faced with stagnant incomes, seeing themselves falling behind those above them on the income scale, and spending their evenings watching *Lifestyles of the Rich and Famous*, what did the average American family do?

First, they worked more. By 2005, families in the middle fifth of the income distribution were working 500 hours, or 12 weeks, longer per year than in 1979. Most of this was due to women's entering paid employment: In 1966, 20 percent of mothers of children under three years old worked outside the home; by 1994, it was 60 percent and rising, though child-care arrangements did not improve much.

Second, they borrowed. And they borrowed bigger and bigger. Household debt rose at an annual rate of 10 percent between the end of 1999 and the third quarter of 2003. Between 1966 and 2006, this debt, adjusted for inflation, rose by almost 3,000 percent. A big hunk of the debt was for mortgages on houses; more and more Americans became homeowners, and houses, unlike families, grew bigger. But, though mortgage debt rose from about one-third of GDP in 1990 to over 80 percent now, home equity (the percentage of the house not owed as mortgage debt) fell from two-thirds of GDP in 1990 to one-half of GDP by 2006; it has, infamously, fallen since. From 1979 on, American politics seemed to be making the nightmare of nineteenth-century classical liberals—irrational populism—come true, as politician after politician called for caps on taxes and increases in spending, the most recent example being George W. Bush. Up until the coming of the widening of the American income distribution, such borrow-and-spend policies had little attraction to the American electorate. That changed as incomes began pulling apart in the 1970s, starting with Howard Jarvis in California in 1979 and reaching full spate with George W. Bush.

Government deficits went from a brief flirtation with zero and even surpluses (which count as savings) at the end of the 1990s into larger and larger deficits in the new century and new administration. Corporations followed suit: Corporate debt shot up by one-third to about $4 trillion between 1997 and 2007. Household debt—mortgages, credit cards, auto and student loans—went from 64 percent of GDP in 1997, to about 100 percent in 2007. Total debt, that is, household, business, and government debt, increased by an entire GDP—a full year's output of the U.S. economy—in the ten years ending in 2007. What assets did Americans borrow against? Only Uncle Sam can borrow on a simple obligation to repay, and only Uncle Sam owns the printing press (as long as he borrows in dollars, that is).

They borrowed on rising asset values. Between 1960 and 1980, the Dow Jones Industrial Average rose from 617 to 824—

much less than zero, once you take inflation into account. But from 1980 to 2000, the average went from 824 to 11,357—more than a tenfold increase. House prices also rose: In 1980, the average house sold for $62,000; in 2006, it went for $245,000, about a fourfold increase, with the big increases coming after 2000. And nearly everyone knew that house prices would continue to rise. The Federal Reserve, aided by China, did its part to help, cutting interest rates after the 2001 dot-com stock market bust, thereby enabling the same monthly payment to carry much higher debt. If tech stocks could no longer do it for them, Americans could still get rich selling their houses to one another.

And they could buy the houses with money borrowed, ultimately, from China. Given the unbalanced flows of goods from China to the United States, a corresponding flow of money from China back to the United States is necessary. If the Chinese produce more than they consume, someone has to buy the stuff, or else production halts. If the United States is to buy more than it produces, someone (China) has to sell it the stuff and lend it the money to buy the goods. The flow of goods is direct: from the manufacturer to Wal-Mart to the consumer. The flows of money, however, are indirect. In order for the individual American homeowner or customer to borrow money, someone has to lend it to him or her. And neither the government of China nor Chinese banks nor Chinese manufacturers do that directly. The flow of money is "intermediated" by the U.S. financial system, which decides who gets to borrow and on what terms, whether for mortgages or credit card debt, for new plants and equipment, or for stock buybacks.

Over the past ten to fifteen years, finance—always an important force in the American economy and in policy making—became a dominant force, perhaps *the* dominant force. It dominated in several reinforcing ways: as the leading growth sector generating swelling incomes and profits; as a substantial contributor to increasing income inequality; as a shaper of business behavior, government policy, and American ideology; and, of course, as the major precipitator of the current financial and economic crisis.

As manufacturing declined as a percentage of what Americans produced—from 21 percent of GDP in 1980 to 14 percent in 2002, finance grew to fill the gap—exactly! As a percentage of what Americans produce, finance rose from 14 percent of GDP in 1980 to 21 percent in 2002. Though manufacturing declined as a proportion of what Americans produce, manufactured goods did not decline significantly as a proportion of what they buy. The difference, of course, is imported, overwhelmingly from East Asia. Finance—not manufacturing, not construction (4 percent of GDP), not the military (5 percent), not even health (16 percent) became the biggest—and fastest-growing—industry in the U.S. economy. And though just about every think tank and politician issued dire warnings about soaring health-care costs, none came forth with programs, or even warnings, to restrain the growth of finance.

By 2002, financial companies had grown to account for over 40 percent of U.S. corporate profits, up from its historical postwar average of between 10 percent and 15 percent. The 40 percent substantially underestimates finance's share of total profits, because significant proportions of the finance industry—venture funds and hedge funds, for example—are typically not organized as corporations. Moreover, the estimates do not usually include profits from the wholly owned finance subsidiaries of industrial firms such as Ford, whose financing division was responsible for all of the automobile company's pretax profits in 2002 and 2003. By 2007, the peak year, finance's profits shot up to represent 47 percent of corporate earnings.

As finance—banking in all its multifarious forms—expanded to become the leading growth sector and the biggest profit generator, remuneration in banking (*earnings* is the preferred euphemism) zoomed up past the other sectors. This had not always been the case; it hadn't been since the late 1920s. From 1948 to 1980, average pay in finance was pretty much the same as in other industries. By 2005, it had increased to double the average pay in the other industries, and bank tellers, of which there are still many, don't get paid very much. The top "earners" in finance, however, pocketed prodigious sums, and the next two, three, or four tiers down also did marvelously well by any standards. They were the pacesetters in America's rush to ever-greater income inequality.

The basic function of the finance system is to round up savings from all over and to channel them to the most productive use. The American financial system dreadfully failed in the performance of its key function, and it was that failure to prudently and responsibly manage the allocation of capital that transformed the fundamentally unsustainable imbalance in America's foreign trade and debt position into a financial and economic crisis of global and historic proportion.

Everyone who could participated. Top Wall Street bankers, Congress, the chairman of the Federal Reserve, the secretaries of the Treasury, the chair of the Securities and Exchange

Commission and other antiregulation government regulators, the press, finance professors at business schools, fresh-grown grassroots mortgage originators, corporate CEOs, and home buyers whose undisguised ignorance rivaled their transparent mendacity. Even honest and often-self-righteous macroeconomists (ourselves as well as the great herd), studying the data that showed productivity in the United States growing far faster than in Europe, grew cautiously convinced that the deregulating, entrepreneurial, free-up-the-market American approach was yielding world-beater results. Recent studies are pointing to the possibility that fundamental difficulties in assigning values for the output of the ballooning financing industry bring into question the data that evidenced much of the superior productivity performance of the U.S. economy in recent, finance-driven years.

Corporations as well as households loaded debt onto equity. New finance theory conveniently explained that nonfinancial corporations could and should borrow money not only for productive investment, but also for buying back their own shares. And they did, in colossal amounts: In 2007, U.S. corporations bought back some $831 billion of their stock, whole-number multiples of their earnings. Of course, the tsunami of corporate borrowings used to buy back stock was a major contributor to rising stock prices and, therefore, to soaring executive incentive-based compensation. It was also a nice business for the bankers, though it left the companies financially weakened should hard times hit and earnings fall.

Finance was the driving force. It had achieved the cultural dominance that so often goes hand-in-hand with economic dominance: its gigantism and ubiquity, its tonic impact on the entire economy, its fabulous success, the sheer gushing of money, its generous funding of elected politicians, its seconding of its top executives to top posts throughout the regulatory apparatus of government, and its simple and powerful message of "let the market work its magic." It was so easy. Nobody had to take responsibility; nobody had to do anything. It all cumulated to finance's full-blown capture of government and culture. How else to explain the tepid opposition to the repeal of the estate tax that hit, at most, the top 2 percent? Though a few tried to sound the alert, day after day, up and down, in and out, in government, in the media, in society itself, no other voices were heard.

There is no limit to the list of what and who went wrong. Incentives were perverse, and this was not totally because of some fit of absentmindedness. Smart, aggressive managers of very big funds of pooled savings were marvelously rewarded by how much they could book as instant profits. This, of course, propelled their decisions toward grabbing for short-term profits and ignoring the costs of longer-term risk. It paid—wildly— to roll the dice on other people's money: One way, you, the manager, win colossal sums. The other way, you take no losses, but other people do, later, after you've cashed out.

The banks were innovative, hiring superbright math students and setting them to create derivatives, derivatives squared, and, ultimately, derivatives cubed. Permitting house mortgages and other debt to be packaged in large bundles and "securitized," the banks made synthetic debt products, thus enabling investors to buy slices (or tranches) of that debt-based synthetic according to taste: higher risk with higher returns; lower risk with lower returns. Mortgages were no longer mainly originated by local banks, which knew the local market, knew the clients, demanded serious documentation of ability to pay on the loan, and kept many of them on their own books. Now, all kinds of new mortgage brokers set up shop, sold mortgages with either insouciance or complicity to buyers who could not qualify under normal scrutiny and who could only pay their debt if the house price would continue to rise and they could flip or refinance against a higher notional value. Many traditional banks adopted the new model. Why carefully check out the borrower? It's arduous and, worse, expensive to do. They wisecracked about Ninja loans—no income, no job, no assets—but wrote them, anyway. Wall Street, where the product was stuffed into long, limp casings and then sliced—and the slices were sliced and etherealized into mathematical functions—did little, if anything, to make sure that its product would pass sanitary codes.

No finance "FDA" insisted on carefully examining and testing innovative financial "foods and drugs." The regulators did not regulate very eagerly, thoroughly, or energetically; they were, as usual but also by design, understaffed. And now they were run at the top by political appointees who were outspoken in their commitment to cut away the morass of regulators and regulations that inhibited market innovation. The attitude of the regulators mirrored that of political Washington: Cut back interference in the market.

It would take a brave banker to refuse to play and watch competitors rake in vast profits not just for a few quick weeks, but year after compounding, marvelous year. He would not only have to be brave and preternaturally confident, but very well defended. The board would clamor for returns at least comparable to competitor banks, and the market would reward their zeal and, presumably, severely punish any lack of it. Chuck Prince, the CEO of Citi, seems to have understood what was going on. He famously remarked: "When the music stops, in terms of liquidity, things will be complicated. But as long as the music is playing, you've got to get up and dance. We're still dancing."

SIX

STATE-LED DEVELOPMENT

Unlike its red-blooded ideological cousin, lemon socialism is not the subject of a vast body of literature. In the West, however, it has resulted in government ownership and control of major hunks of economies.

Coming out of the Depression and World War II, Western European governments found themselves by accident and design with controlling interests in substantial parts of their national financial and industrial sectors. Some of this was deliberate: the belief by left-of-center governments that their proper role was to own and control the "commanding heights" of the economy. More of this, however, was generally accidental—some losing enterprises that were deemed too big to fail and some enterprises for which privates were unwilling to invest in expansion on a sufficient scale. In Italy, for example, the government owned the largest banks; the railways; the radio and TV stations; and monopolies or major firms in steel, oil, electric power, telephones, cigarettes, aircraft and airlines, toll highways, insurance, autos, electrical equipment, and even pasta. Something similar existed in Spain, a heritage of Franco. Giant state-owned sectors were to be found not only in countries with Fascist histories, but in other countries as well. In France, for reasons of lemon socialism, full red-blooded socialism, and some postwar confiscation of collaborationists' companies (Renault), as late as 1981, the state owned banks that accounted for about 85 percent of all deposits, and monopolies or major companies in insurance, railways, autos, railroads, tobacco, radio and television broadcasting, electricity, gas, telephone, maritime shipping, electronics and many others. Despite, because of, or with no relation whatever to this dominant economic role for the state, France modernized and grew quite as fast as its awesome neighbor, Germany—to the surprise of the world and especially the French themselves. And state-controlled firms set the pace and led the way.

For the past twenty-five years, however, these Western European countries, along with much of the rest of the globe, have been actively privatizing their state holdings. They have reduced government ownership. They have pared back their governments' direct efforts to influence market outcomes.

Privatization and the dismantling of active industrial policy even took root in Continental Europe, as the English like to call it, where it was aided by a particular and powerful force. The European Union's drive to create a single European market was a deep, sustained, and far-reaching effort to establish conditions for the free flow of all economic factors across the European economic space, not just product, but labor, capital, and management control, and the elimination of institutional and policy barriers to freer and more vigorous competition across national borders. This translated into the persistent dismantling of the principal instruments of national industrial regulatory policy—subsidization, protection, preferred procurement, and artful standards, rules, and regulations.

Eliminating obstacles to the free flow of capital and competition set Brussels cutting away at state ownership, control, and attempts to influence outcomes. In the 1990s, the demonstrable fact that even France had privatized its companies and pulled back from actively and systematically intervening to affect industrial outcomes boosted international acceptance of the U.S.-U.K. message: Leave it to the market. The brilliantly flaunted prosperity of the U.S. economy—and even the long-ailing British economy—during the 1990s and the early 2000s clinched the case.

The current crisis is beginning with a worldwide reaction against what are perceived to be both the excesses and the defects of neoliberalism, the "leave it to the market and get the state's hands out" ideology or universal policy prescription that had been so triumphant. Whenever and however it ends, it is likely to end with governments—once again—unafraid to use the substantial ownership stakes they will have amassed in a host of distressed national firms in finance and industry. In their efforts to stimulate their economies, governments are likely to try to be strategically as well as macroeconomically smart and to shift their economies toward bright and even virtuous new directions like clean energy, which is seen by all governments and investors as huge and good.

Each government will be tempted and pressured to use its leverage for the national interest, as well as many special interests: to support and strengthen big, distressed industries and to promote investments in new industries. A move by one country will push others to rush to the same, crowding the exit ways. After all, if the United States, Germany, or Korea bails out its auto parts makers or its banks, insurers, or airlines, then shouldn't France or Italy also do so? If they don't, they risk letting their companies and workers pay the price of American or German market-distorting policy. In the current crisis, all of the industrial countries have lots of big lemons— offices and factories owned by both national and foreign companies in sectors that had worldwide overcapacity before demand suddenly collapsed. Ensuring their operations and survival in one country squeezes the other countries' lemons all the harder, and around it goes.

Ships are sitting empty. Prices for ocean shipping have plummeted as volumes have fallen, while costs are overwhelmingly fixed. Orders for new ships spiked during the shipping boom of the past few years. Now orders are being canceled as quickly as possible. Shipyards are in trouble. The Chinese government is responding by pushing its shipping companies to buy new ships and keep its shipyards operating and their huge workforces employed. But this further depresses business not just for shipyards in other countries, but also for shippers for whom the launching of even more competition means yet lower prices and bigger losses. Maersk, one of the biggest ocean shippers, is a Danish company, but how can Denmark or Greece compete with China in a subsidy race? Something similar is happening with aluminum producers. In the short term, where a company winds up in the triage process has less to do with better products and greater efficiency and more to do with which companies have more aggressive, more agile, and simply more government support.

Although *companies* may be the conventional category for thinking and, especially, talking about these issues, it may be the wrong unit. In autos, for example, companies now operate global production portfolios spread out across many countries. So the target unit is less the company—GM or Daimler-Benz— than specific facilities and activities, such as plants, design centers, and those of suppliers. The transformation of national champions into multinationals complicates industrial policy.

Defensive industrial policy—that is, stepping in to support failing industries, or ranching lemons—is not all there is. There are two other forms: John Stuart Mill's "infant industry" of endeavoring to shape market outcomes to shift national economic development onto a new and higher trajectory by promoting national firms in specific sectors, and its converse endeavoring to shape others' national economic development in directions that support one's own development goals.

Americans like to say scornfully that industrial policy is about "governments picking winners." Picking winner industries is not that hard—even for governments. Most countries trying to climb the ladder of quality and industrial sophistication through selective promotion compiled pretty much the same lists at the same time. Even at the leading edge of the technological frontier, the industries that governments are tempted to promote are largely the same ones picked by the analysts and brokers at investment firms such as Merrill Lynch, Nomura, or Rothschild's. In the past, the picks would have been semiconductors, computers, mobile technology, or biotechnology. Right now, yet again, governments and analysts alike are all picking clean tech, nanotech, and biotech. Picking "winner industries" is not the hard part; winning is. It is difficult to create actual winners, companies that develop into successful competitors. It is easy to establish a national champion company in a winning industry and have it develop into an inefficient, cash-draining zombie—witness Brazil's and France's thirty-year losing efforts in computers or, indeed, the Japanese Fifth Generation computer project. Even the venture capital firm of Kleiner-Perkins, a great Silicon Valley winner picker, appears to have on net failed to increase its investors' money in its picks since 1998 except for one single company: Google.

But sometimes these efforts succeed. Brazil built a national champion that, after decades of military subsidy, now holds an honorable niche in regional jets: Embraer. Japan targeted electronics and succeeded in climbing to a leading position in that giant industry. A bit later, Taiwan and Korea did the same. And France also targeted nuclear energy, space rocket launchers, commercial aviation (eventually, Airbus at the European scale), and supertrains. It succeeded, for better or worse, in being a world leader in each of those advanced industries. All of these not only required patient and massive government support, but are also, by their very nature, impossible to launch to scale without such support. They are different—in kind—from Twitter, Federal Express, Google, Countrywide, Wal-Mart, Disney, or Apple. Now China is trying to climb up that greasy, crowded, and possibly buckling pole.

State-led economic development by the developmental states of East Asia such as Japan and Korea has been a wonder of the world, cutting decades if not generations off the predicted times for their emergence as prosperous, modern economies. Governments all over the world seek to emulate these extraordinary development successes. Now that the financial crisis has freed them from the fetters and blinders of the Washington consensus and the neoliberal ideology, the governments will attempt to deploy their market-rigging economic instruments— their money, their sovereign wealth funds, their stimulus packages, along with the various nonmonetary instruments at their disposal—to accelerate their rise to prosperity. Will they succeed? Probably not. Strategies and institutions that work well in some times and places fail catastrophically in others. But they will try.

The great successes in industrial policy were achieved by countries that didn't have to invent their future but only had to catch up with it—what Thorstein Veblen famously first called the "advantages of backwardness." Japan's industrial planners could select an industry to target from a set of fully studied candidates and later, from the vantage of a higher rung on the development ladder, could similarly select the next ones: first steel and ships, then machinery and autos, then electronics. The Japanese succeeded in all of these, one after the other, beyond their wildest initial ambitions. But they didn't do quite so well with technologies and industries that had not yet been invented elsewhere or had yet to take proper industrial form, such as advanced computing, biotech, and Internet plumbing and applications. Nonetheless, many governments will probably have a go at another round of smart industrial policy. After all, the same list of big next new things is on everyone's desk. And now the governments have the money plus the compelling need to "stimulate" their wracked economies.

Consider an earlier pair of very big, well-known next new things—commercial jet aircraft and semiconductors. They encompass technology; just about all new (nonbiological) technologies go into big jets, and semiconductors go into, or into the production of, most everything. Though rarely acknowledged in good economist company, at no time—from their first origins through the present moment—in the relatively short histories of both of those industries was some government not intervening to affect competitive outcomes and the location of value added. And it was the United States that secured early dominance in both those industries. Would it really be shocking to learn that China might take a run at a lead position in photovoltaics or wind turbines, or stake itself to a place in regional and then big commercial jets, an industry now shared by Boeing and Airbus?

Will these likely efforts, backed by the new redistribution of the money, threaten the absolute, or relative, position of the American economy? Quite possibly yes.

The danger is not that countries with money will purchase American companies (directly or through their national companies)—which they will—and make off with the "shareholder value," which they won't. The real danger has to do with where the spillovers of innovation go.

Recall that innovation has over the past fifty years provided more than half of all real economic growth in the United States and that almost all of the benefits from invention and innovation spilled outside the innovating company. The classic examples are AT&T and Xerox, whose UNIX project and Palo Alto Research Center (PARC), respectively provided proof-of-concept running code for almost the entire software industry. But if AT&T made a dollar off UNIX, we would be very surprised. And Xerox lost a fortune at PARC. There is a story—probably false—that when Apple was jostling Microsoft, Steve Jobs complained to Bill Gates about Microsoft's copying Apple's interface: "It's like you broke into my house and took my TV set!" "That's not true, Steve," was Gates's apocryphal reply. "We had a rich neighbor named Xerox, and we both took Xerox's TV set—you just took it first." There is nothing immoral or illegal or destructive and a great deal that is advantageous for long-run economic growth in the flow of knowledge from firm to firm in and beyond Silicon Valley and other such communities. Communities of innovation and of engineering practice are how leading-edge economic growth happens. Such flows of knowledge have always happened since before the philosopher Thales of Miletus is supposed to have made some suggestions for improving the efficiency of the olive presses of Caria. Johannes Gutenberg's invention of movable type quickly spread across and then beyond Mainz; Ford's innovation of the assembly line quickly benefited GM, GE, and Westinghouse and then spread around the world.

Usually, at least in the past, the spillovers have tended to cluster, at least initially, in tight physical propinquity to the actual invention and innovation; regional industrial growth poles have been a powerful force since the first one was established in Lancashire at the start of the nineteenth century (or perhaps in Florence at the start of the eleventh). But will regional propinquity be that essential in our future of always-on, ubiquitous, instantaneous, worldwide communications? And what will happen when governments with ownership stakes in firms think that it would be nice if they would tune things so that the spillovers happen not where the operations are currently located, but rather where the government would prefer the spillovers to be? And this growth can be shifted. Money helps. It can try to shift many things, including the generators of yet more money. It can take totally new technologies out of the start-up companies that create them and attempt to shift them back home for next stage development into full-scale production, growth, and development into yet newer products and processes. Some such efforts will succeed. Most will probably fail. But when they fail, they will still have inflicted damage on the innovating economy. And a great many attempts will be made. Like the shift in political power represented by the relocation of the money, this is an unpleasant possibility to contemplate, especially from the heartland of innovation.

Defensive industrial policy—lemon socialism—can have a similar growth-shifting effect. Think of American football. The helmet was defensive at first, to protect players' brains. But it then developed into the hard-shell helmet, an offensive battering ram. Distressed traditional industries do not consist entirely of petrified wood. They often contain high-growth, high-value bits and technologies that will generate substantial growth in sales, jobs, skills, and knowledge. These bits can be moved to a new home, leaving the aging hulk in the United States. And you don't have to close down the plant and ship it overseas: It can all happen at the margin, in the location of production for the next product, or the location of the next factory, or the decision on where to close excess capacity. Lots of factors—not just efficiency—can influence that choice: "We will bail you out and plough money into the plant right here, but we can't have our money going into supporting jobs at some foreign plant" is a governmental refrain that locates present and future economic activities, not just the dead weight of permanent losers. Politicians feel that using their taxpayers' money to subsidize jobs in other countries "isn't justified," as France's outspoken president, Nicolas Sarkozy, said point-blank. Most political leaders, especially in countries with traditions of free-market rhetoric, don't dare to speak so matter-of-factly.

What to do? One bad possible reaction is to vet all foreign purchases that could be of concern to the United States not just for reasons of military security—as we already do—but also for economic security. The U.S. government would have to discriminate, on a case-by-case basis, among foreign investors and even look through their American partners to identify them. This would not be easy even for a Korea, Japan, or France, which have well-established bureaucratic capabilities and which know the game. It would be especially difficult for the United States. The American government should never try to micromanage; it cannot. It has political and administrative structures that, compared with these countries, are particularly ill suited to vet foreign investors and investments, one by one, to differentiate among individual cases—not broad, legally defined categories The attempt by Dubai Ports World to purchase P&O port facility operations on the East Coast of the United States produced a political furor at the highest

levels. Congress and the press rose up in outrage. The great
and the good swiftly portrayed this reaction as ominous, xeno-
phobic protectionism. But it was not a simple case of protectionism, of wanting to keep foreigners out, and most, though
alas, probably not all, of the congressional outbursters knew
it. It was a complex case of preferring one foreigner to another.
Those against the purchase did not want one most-acceptable
corporate foreigner, the venerable British company P&O, to
sell a U.S. asset that looked as though it could have security
implications to a particular other foreigner. This foreigner was
owned and controlled by the government of Dubai, a hot spot
for all kinds of transactions and comings and goings not all of
which involved hot U.S. architects and Wall Street salesmen.
It was a political effort to discriminate against an Arab government, not foreign investors in general. It was a security
concern—wise or foolish.

The United States was not able to handle this sort of question deftly. We magnified it outrageously, transformed it into
another kind of question, and burst it into fiasco. You can't do
that sort of thing on an ongoing basis. And it is much harder
to handle when the question concerns not the outright purchase
of a company or facility, but the adroit, day-to-day transfer of
the economic potential of an innovation.

The problem is not foreign ownership per se. It cannot be,
because ineluctably, there will be more and more of it. After
all, they have the money. All classes of our assets—real estate,
government and corporate bonds, minority holdings of corporate stock, and control of companies—will shift to foreign
owners. Real estate poses zero problems despite the fearful

cries that followed the Japanese purchase of Rockefeller Center when Japan, briefly, had the money. You can't pick up a building and move it. Nor do bonds and truly minority stock holdings pose problems: All you can really do is buy them or sell them. But some controlling interests in some companies might, sometimes, pose some real difficulties. The problem is how to handle a nearly endless series of who, what, and how. The prognosis for an effective U.S. response here is poor, possibly hopeless.

There are, however, calming considerations. First, this is nothing new. America has already been through all this and survived it. All by itself, albeit with some assists from Asian governments, the market system has been doing a rather fine job of encouraging American companies to relocate substantial portions of the benefits of innovation to Asia. Second, most sovereign wealth funds do not come with this danger. Funds from countries like Norway do not do that sort of thing, but then again, there are not many Norways. The giant pots of money in the Gulf don't pose that kind of threat. No one, themselves included, seriously thinks that the Gulf states can relocate innovations back home and sustain and harvest their growth potential. With the Europeans, there is a lively back-and-forth in the location of technology, ideas, plants, and innovative people. It has been very roughly in balance with few problems on the horizon.

The Asian manufacturing nations, trying to move up into higher and higher technology and value added, are successful industrial-policy countries that seem highly unlikely to kick the habit, especially now that they have a fine new tool: cash, vast piles of wealth that need at some point to be moved out of dollars to be shielded from the risks of substantial exchange-rate depreciation. One shift will be into strategic investments by Asian sovereign wealth funds or national companies with access to that money to try to relocate the locus of development.

Money is just one power available to those governments, especially China. There is also the power of access to, and success in, the Chinese market. For example, there is Huawei's use of what at first seemed to Cisco to be Cisco's own technology, or the awaited denouement of China's experiment with a European very fast train that ludicrously zips from Shanghai airport to Shanghai. Will a foreign company get the contract for the real runs—beginning with Shanghai to Beijing—and hold on to its technology, or will the real runs have a Chinese company either providing something that strongly resembles the European (or Japanese) technology, or as a major technology-sharing and market-sharing partner?

And what if the Chinese simply copy the technology? Or, through deals that can't be refused—a big piece of the world's best and biggest market—squeeze the technology for the very fast train out of the Europeans? How could they fight back? The European train makers have had, to say the least, very strong assists from their governments. Should the German or French governments choose to defend them, what could they really do? Threaten the Chinese with some kind of retaliation? Doubtful. After all, they have Airbuses to sell, and China is the biggest likely buyer, and those same governments are deeply involved in Airbus. It is not at all clear that they could do much of anything, except work out some kind of reasonable deal: OK, you make off with the technology, use it at home, but you give us half of the China market. And what about China exporting it? Economics talks a lot about market power, but little about the power of a market if you control access to it.

The interventionist approach has a long history. Industrial policy is a whispered word in Japan, a common usage in France, and a portmanteau pejorative in America. There are major differences in how governments tried to promote their winners. Japan and Korea are shining examples of long-term, large-scale success of very active, sectorally focused industrial policy. Over time, they succeeded in willfully changing the composition of their economies and the structures of their comparative advantage. Japan didn't invent its way into electronics, nor did Korea. Government targeted the industries, protected infant firms, supported them by steering lots of patient capital and customers their way, and kept at it for years. The same government attention propelled the development of the nations' enormous and enormously successful steel, shipbuilding, machine tool, and auto industries. France, a more open economy, a proudly high-wage establishment, and a more graceful player, made a similar sustained effort at government promotion of key industries. And despite this effort, or in part because of it, France is still high up on anyone's list of the richest countries in the world.

The best and biggest successes occurred when determined, strong, and well-organized governments could plainly see what they were aiming at. Industrial policy that aims at capturing the next new thing is, however, a fundamentally different game from catch-up. It requires very different and much less well-understood capabilities.

Targeting "industries of the future"—not just your future but the world's—is precisely where clarity is hard to come by, and when it comes, it is sometimes merely will-o'-the-wisp. Fusion power is the clearest example: For the past two generations, the industry of the future; most likely, for the next two also. It is all about uncertainty—not simple risk. It is not about playing the odds with portfolio theory; it is about not knowing the odds. But it is not a game lacking eager players; the payoffs, if you can snatch and hold them, are huge. It is generally accepted that when a government directs its money and efforts at the level of scientific research, in clear-cut precommercial stages—that is, basic research—it is very much treated as the right and proper role of government. The support is considered infrastructural, like roads, bridges, and education. But this is a costly, slow, and very uncertain business. Even if there are commercially valuable results, it is now much harder than it used to be to hold those benefits in the national economy.

One alternative approach is simply to come in late, after the scientific uncertainty has crystallized out, and seek to gain a good chunk of the economic benefit of innovation—no matter where the innovation occurs—and plant it for large-scale growth into the home economy. Many companies in innovative businesses such as biotech or electronics have set up research centers in places such as Scandinavia, Israel, and, of course, Silicon Valley to get their noses and fingers into clusters of innovative activity. Eager countries with a well-developed industrial policy apparatus can do the same thing, most often through their own companies, which they can always back with steroidal doses of money, but also, should they choose, as direct cash investments from their wealth funds.

Innovation is generally not as mysterious or idiosyncratic as it is so often portrayed, the work of an isolated, driven, lonely genius. Rather, it happens in clusters, groups, or communities of innovators busying around some major, enabling scientific development that is well known globally. The innovations that open commercial applications happen within these small communities of innovation and slosh around its constituent people, institutions, and firms. No one can really know who will hit the winning combination, but it is a fair bet that someone will, most likely more than one. At this point, something more than luck, inspiration, and perseverance will count: Money is a likely candidate. That is why venture capital firms have such redundant portfolios: One firm in this charged space will likely hit it; we just can't know which. And deep money can help one firm out-invest and prevail over its competitors.

This way of thinking about innovation and its transformation into industry is a kind of Silicon Valley view: Success comes from high-energy, new firms full of kids with stock options—kids who snort pizza and coke and rock koans after midnight at their work stations. Imagination, ingenuity, and speed are all-important; massive amounts of patient capital don't much count. Sometimes this view fits reality, especially when what is involved is pushing around bits, not atoms, that is, low capital costs to enter the market, low capital costs for expansion, huge economies of scale (or exponential network economies), and even lock-ins.

But quite often, the next new thing doesn't come about this way, and can't. France's list of big-time industrial policy successes illustrates this other route. None of them—nuclear energy, big commercial jet aircraft, space rockets and satellites, and high-speed trains—unlike, say, personal computers, MP3 players, Google, Craigslist, or hybrid cars, can be developed into something big without extensive and prolonged government involvement. By extensive, we mean not just government financing of research and development over many years, but also government organization of a market, government or government-controlled entities directly providing a launch market at the necessary scale, which is huge, and government creating the rules and regulations necessary for that market's operation. Launching all of these new industries required not the lightweight speed, smarts, and agility of the Silicon Valley model, but this kind of deep and extensive government incubation. And all of them got it. And each of them—except the last, very high-speed trains—was developed and initially dominated, not by France, but by America.

AMERICAN INDUSTRIAL POLICY

America doesn't "do" industrial policy. We don't like it. We don't approve of others doing it. We think that when they do, it hurts us and usually ends up hurting them as well. Furthermore, we're just not set up to do it. Unlike the situation in some other countries, the institutional design deeply embedded in American political, legal, and administrative structures is quite unsuitable for selective, discretionary, and sustained intervention by government bureaucrats. Ideological conviction and an overall judgment on results reinforce this position. Government is, and ought to be, the referee in the market game, not the coach, linemen, and quarterback. In brief, the American view as expressed in its domestic politics, in its positions in international forums, and in the discourse of its economists is that industrial policy is largely a form of cheating. At best it unfairly free-rides on the overall system, and usually it backfires and ensnares the intervening government into taxing the healthy parts of its economy to support losers. We don't do it.

Proper Europeans older than fifty will eagerly tell you that this insistently proclaimed American view is disingenuous. Americans didn't call it industrial policy; they called it defense.

There is considerable truth to this smirking assertion. In the post–World War II period, the Department of Defense (DoD) put into place its huge and permanent budget; its daunting discretion in determining its technological and industrial needs; its extended time horizon, replete with twenty-year projects; its cadres of well-trained technology bureaucrats in special technology-industrial development agencies such as DARPA (Defense Advanced Research Projects Agency); and its family of technologically sophisticated, if not quite market-responsive, supplier firms such as Raytheon, Lockheed, Boeing, United Technologies, GE, General Dynamics, Collins, and Harris. DoD's industrial activities were complemented by related agencies such as the Atomic Energy Commission, the commission's successors, and NASA. This Pentagon economy was protected from economics as well as politics. Economics stopped at the Maginot Line: The defense sector was bracketed and removed from the usual concerns for market performance and efficiency. It was, in many ways, a separate economy operating by separate rules and criteria, and concern with optimal market outcomes was certainly not one of them.

From 1955 through 1985, military spending in the United States averaged about 7.5 percent of GDP. No other non-Soviet bloc country came even close; France was second, averaging about half the U.S. rate, and Japan about one-seventh.

Determining or even opining on whether defense spending was a boon or a bane for the U.S. economy is not our concern. But we do assert that it played a powerful and consequential role in promoting specific technological/industrial capabilities that developed into significant areas of American competitive dominance in the world economy. The Pentagon did not set out to reform the U.S. economy, certainly not with the goal of making it more competitive internationally. Instead, DoD set out to supply its own, ever-evolving technological requirements, ambitions, and dreams.

Consider several significant examples of Pentagon industrial policy. Examples should not automatically be dismissed as mere anecdotes. Sometimes, they are economically consequential in their own right, and industrial policy, an ongoing effort at sectoral selection and upgrading, is precisely about consequential "examples." The Pentagon's early role in promoting U.S. industrial capabilities in commercial jet aircraft is not merely illustrative, but also economically very significant in its own right, opening the way for the United States to seize world dominance in a critical industry. It is also the target for venting European "truth squads" each time Boeing and the

U.S. government bring charges that Airbus is hugely subsidized and constitutes unfair competition according to international norms and treaties. After artful denials that Airbus is somehow subsidized, which, of course, it was and at fabulous amounts, the Europeans climb onto firmer ground and charge that the Boeing 707 commercial airliner, the plane that gave Boeing market dominance, is really the Air Force K-135 tanker with windows. It came down the same assembly line, which was built by U.S. Air Force money; it was shaped by the same specialty machine tools, which could fashion specialty metals into twelve-dimensional Brancusi-like shapes and which were developed with U.S. Air Force money; it was powered by jet engines also developed—at whopping costs—under air force contracts that extended back even to the developments in metallurgy needed to make those engines. Boeing's commercial jet business—the world's dominant leader until Airbus's long climb to parity—is a spin-off from, or an application of, the Pentagon's technology and procurement policy.

The transistor was not invented by some kids in a Silicon Valley garage; it came out of Bell Labs, the sheltered research laboratory of the government-regulated telephone monopoly, AT&T, also a defense contractor. The appeal of semiconductors instead of big, hot, forever-blowing-out vacuum tubes in the tight cockpit of a fighter plane is obvious, once you see the technology and have it in hand. The early development of the semiconductor into something that was a useful, reliable product that could be produced at industrial scale was powered by DoD procurement contracts. Even the proliferation of small, competing semiconductor firms in what became Silicon Valley is in part due to DoD insistence on dual sourcing and cross-licensing: The Pentagon was not going to count on the success, or even the survival, of start-up firms. The breathtaking improvements in semiconductor performance à la Moore's Law and the development of myriad applications, like desktops, laptops, cell phones, appliances, automotives, machinery—everything!—owes little, indeed nothing, to DoD. These cascading advancements were driven by the competitive structures and energies of Silicon Valley and later, of course, by the Japanese, who availed themselves handsomely of the transistor technology for which, at the technology's infancy, the U.S. Department of Justice forced wide licensing.

Computing followed a similar soaring trajectory. U.S. producers—and, just as important, users—forged well ahead of everyone else, thanks in no small measure to powerful and very early assistance from DoD. We all learned how the first computers—versions of ENIAC—filled enormous rooms and required nursing staffs of dozens of people constantly running about, replacing popped vacuum tubes. Who would buy one of those monsters? Pretty much only Uncle Sam: the Weather Bureau, the Census, and, of course, DoD. Defense efforts to spur computing and to create a computer industry, or capability, as the military conceived of it, extended way upstream; DoD even created and supported pioneering university programs in computer science. This was truly bold and farsighted industrial policy that paid off royally for DoD's own mission of deploying computing power vastly superior to that of any foreign rivals, and for the U.S. economy.

The Internet had a maiden name: DARPA-net. Created by DARPA, the network was designed to deal with a problem that the agency posed to itself: how to assure communications if the Russkies nuked Chicago, a giant node for telephone, as well as rail lines. DARPA's solution was to create a communications network with no indispensible central nodes, the basic architecture of the Internet. At first, the DARPA-net linked major government laboratories such as Los Alamos and some major research universities, such as MIT, Caltech, and Berkeley. This was the giant beta test. It was also, for those few early years, a uniquely great place to buy a used Volvo or a golden retriever, and to locate a sabbatical rental or swap. The network then grew and grew and grew at a pace and to an extent that no one had ever imagined. A few additional innovations were needed before it evolved into the Internet that we all know: the browser, which was invented at the U.S. government's Fermi lab in Illinois (no locus of entrepreneurial firms) and then picked off by Jim Clark, a Silicon Valley entrepreneur, rechristened Mosaic, and floated on the stock market for a fabulous return as Netscape. Similarly, the hypertext markup language—HTML, or click to link—came not out of the entrepreneurial sector, but from CERN, the European atomic energy laboratory located astride the French Swiss border near the evocatively named town, Fernet-Voltaire.

The modest microwave oven, an example of much smaller spin-offs, came out of Raytheon, a defense contractor then specializing in radar. One day, Raytheon engineers realized that you could cook with radar. Thus was born the "radar range," as it was first called. Almost twenty years later, after a try at licensing, Raytheon went into commercial production as Amana, with a product designed for home use. Soon thereafter, the Japanese took dominance. This highlights one of the weaknesses in DoD industrial policy: It was aimed at DoD's needs, not those of the economy. The Pentagon was necessarily aware of broader economic possibilities, but spin-offs were the route out of the defense economy into the commercial economy. For development and production, DoD typically relied on its family of contractors, mostly giant, technologically sophisticated firms like Lockheed, General Dynamics, and Raytheon, all of whose internal workings were geared to the Pentagon's way of doing business: rigorous and costly testing and documentation; heavy, lengthy, and not-very-cost-sensitive procurement procedures and cycles; and, usually, cost-plus pricing.

On its own turf—competing with other militaries, especially the Soviets—DoD was unbeatable, but it was not aiming at producing products and firms that were well adapted to competition in civilian markets vigorously contested by the agile. For rockets, satellites, jet engines, aircraft, mainframes, and supercomputing (the latter two now quaint terms), this was not a problem. It became a problem, a serious one, in electronics. By the 1980s, spin-off was losing the race to "spin-on" (i.e., sourcing from the commercial sector) in electronics, the critical defense technology. The commercial sector innovated, embodied innovation, and made it reliable much faster than did the defense sector; commercial entities produced at vastly greater volumes and at far lower prices. DoD increasingly had to source vital components of military systems—semiconductors, lasers, flat panel displays, optical storage, etc.—from the civilian economy. Increasingly, this meant relying on Japanese, not American, mass producers.

In 1986, DoD went public in its Defense Sciences Board report, "The Use of Commercial Components in Military Equipment." The document revealed that commercial electronics such as computers, radios, and displays were just as durable, even in harsh environments, one to three times more advanced, two to ten times cheaper, five times faster to acquire, and more reliable than their military equivalents. For the foreseeable future, the report concluded, "commercial-to-military 'spin-ons' are likely to boom while military-to-commercial 'spin-offs' decline." Even beyond electronics, DoD's spin-off industrial policy was beginning to show its structural defects or, more precisely, the commercial ironies of its successes. In the 1950s and 1960s, DoD had sponsored the creation of very advanced, numerically controlled machine tools for use in aircraft production. And it got them. But, in doing so, it had also shaped the American machine tool industry. By the 1980s, the defects of this unrivaled excellence were becoming apparent in the steep decline of that industry in the face of foreign competition. DoD-inspired technology was proving to be too expensive and far too complicated to operate under normal industrial conditions than the simpler, cheaper machines that came out of Japan's industrial policy, which focused precisely on tools for ordinary industrial applications, or German high-end, factory-friendly machine tools.

Like an intelligent military recognizing the limits of its forces, DoD has continued to push ahead on the spin-on, going so far as to establish its own venture firm in Silicon Valley to monitor, access, and assist interesting new technologies in start-up companies. Truly new technologies such as computing, biotechnology, or even, long ago, electric motors take considerable time to move, at scale, from laboratory to market; twenty years is rather a norm. It is possible that spin-offs from relatively recent DoD projects will find important, driving roles in the American economy in the near future. But the contrast between the commercial successes of spin-offs from DoD projects of the 1950s and 1960s and those of the 1980s and 1990s brings American assertions that we don't do industrial policy a lot closer to God's honest truth.

SEVEN

Conclusion: Other Countries' Money

After almost a century, the United States no longer has the money. It is gone, and it is not likely to return in the foreseeable future. The American standard of living will decline relative to the rest of the industrialized and industrializing world: For the past ten years, America has been consuming more than it produces and living beyond its means by borrowing. For American households, borrowing will no longer be an easy option.

The United States will lose power and influence. Its government will no longer be able to act the role of the unique, multidimensional superpower that pays attention to other governments only when it wishes. Whether this should be rued or applauded by Americans and by other peoples is an open question. Money is a key fact of power. When a great nation becomes a massive debtor, it loses considerable freedom of action, and that is a fact with consequence. The United States will remain a world power and, perhaps, the leading nation; it just will no longer be able to be the boss. That it will be constrained in ways it has not been in the past is a huge change that will take getting used to, and not just for America. As bosses go, America's sway has been relatively easy for nearly a century, which has permitted many other rich and potentially powerful nations such as Japan and the larger European states to avoid the bother of growing up; to enjoy the comfort of having someone else in charge; and to indulge, like normal adolescents, the opportunity to blame and gripe. Once the realization sinks in that Uncle can no longer quite handle it all—and it might take a while for that to happen—anxiousness is likely to replace dissatisfied restlessness.

The way governments run their economies, at both the national and the international level, is likely to change. The neoliberal prescription—free up the market and let it rip—has been triumphant for the past twenty-five years in the outside world as well as in the United States. But this approach will not regain its unchallenged dominance, though there will be heroic efforts by the king's men and horses, too—financial, business, and government leaders—to bring about the rehabilitation of the neoliberal model. Nevertheless, in the future, governments are likely to take a more active role intervening in their economies to affect market outcomes than they have over the past generation. They will do this in part because of the pressure of rescuing their own economies from the economic and financial crisis that is punishing all of them, in part because of the new freedom to act opened up by the breakdown of the neoliberal system, and in part because other governments are acting—and if they do not do, they risk having done to them. And the governments that accumulate enormous pools of money in their reserves, in their sovereign wealth funds, and in the companies they directly and indirectly own or control will attempt to play an important role in the fate of not just their own economies but also those of others.

The U.S. economy will recover from this narrowly averted depression. So will the global economy. But neither will simply snap back to its previous level and, more important, form. The neoliberal order as it evolved required that one giant economy, America, be the balance wheel: able and willing to reliably and regularly import more than it exported so that others countries could (1) export vastly more than they imported, (2) shift labor out of subsistence farming into much more productive industry, (3) invest the proceeds, and (4) do it again to grow their industrial production and prowess. Done enough and done right, the process would eventually create a big enough and rich enough domestic market to absorb much, though not all, of other countries' vast production of world-market-type goods. The United States is unlikely to be able to play that role to anything like the extent it previously did. And there is no indication of another great economy and political entity stepping in.

The role has its attractions. You get to spend more than you produce. You are not constrained like the others. You just print money and use it—for consumption, for political influence, and for the sheer feeling of power and pride. And you don't have to keep within your means, as the international economic system quickly obliges all other countries. An "exorbitant privilege" Charles de Gaulle called it over a generation ago. It was a key complement to dominant military, cultural, and political power. But it had its costs.

Importing far more than you export does mean weakening, year after year, your industries that compete with those imports—in the American case, a broad swath of industries, from machine tools to electronics. The communities of engineering practice and innovative technological development do move and emerge elsewhere as you shift labor from real engineering, which calculates stresses in materials and quantum tunneling in doped semiconductors, into financial engineering, which calculates delta-hedge decay and vega convexity for synthetic securities. It also means that you must create more and more debt so that other nations have the dollars to accumulate and not balance their trade—and yours.

Of course, this sort of thing cannot be sustained forever. The Asian export-led growth model must—over time—transform itself to domestic consumption and prosperity models. The American borrow-and-import model will also have to shift—again, this takes considerable time—to a model of consume-at-the level-you-produce. And the need to keep the confidence of those who have the money that their money is well placed in the United States serves as a constraint on U.S. policy in a way that it has never been before.

In the United States, as in most other nations, the direction of growth has regularly been reshaped by government policy. The American West was opened by government-subsidized railroads. This was easy for the U.S. government to accomplish: It didn't have to budget money; it just had to give away land—which it owned in unimaginable extent—and the railroad tracks would make that land valuable. The railway companies could then sell it and pay for the railroad construction and then some. Opening the West through railroad building seemed and was an obvious economic policy objective. Most government-propelled growth sectors seem obvious and have broad support as a goal; they are not chosen whimsically. Railroads to the West created a set of new leading sectors, not just the railroads themselves and their supplier industries such as steel, which soared in scale and leaped forward in technological sophistication of both product and process, but also farms, mines, and cities. This induced growth was the big economic fact and the form of development.

After World War II, it was the government mortgage and highway-subsidy-fueled growth of the suburbs that reshaped the landscape and the economy: roads, autos, oil, schools, shopping centers, and houses filled with new appliances and furniture. Government insurance of mortgage financing made home ownership possible for the working and middle classes. The Defense Highway Act built the roads that laid out those houses in their suburban form, which then required the autos that filled those roads. Add the ever-full trough of the defense sector, and together they shaped the U.S. economy and drove it for its fastest and longest growth ever. Lobbyists—auto, oil, construction—loved these policies, and Americans did, too.

In the past fifteen years, the United States has half-consciously reshaped its economy. The country shifted some 7 percent of its GDP out of manufacturing and added some 7 percent of GDP in the expansion of finance, insurance, and real estate transactions. Finance became the fastest-growing and biggest sector and the biggest generator of jobs and incomes (if not exactly, we are finding out, products of comparably real-use value).

This shift, too, was not a simple, spontaneous act. True, the accumulations of U.S. debt held by foreigners had to go some-place within the American economy. But there were other places besides growing the financial sector where it could have ended up. Sustained government policies largely of omission (deregulation, "de-enforcement" of existing regulations, and "de-extension" of regulatory regimes to not cover new financial products and growing institutions) enabled and encouraged the growth in finance and what it funded. And Americans as consumers did not cut back on manufactured goods, but im-ported them, and the imports were ultimately financed by ac-cumulations of foreign-held debt. This economic form is one to which the United States and its complicitous foreign partners cannot and should not try to return.

Right now, American policy makers—President Obama, Larry Summers, Tim Geithner, and especially Ben Bernanke at the Fed—are scrambling to put back the shattered pieces of the financial system and to pump cash into the economy to offset the spending that households are not doing. Similar ef-forts are being undertaken in other countries, big and small. The task is massive, delicate, and parlous.

But this massive effort is an attempt to put Humpty Dumpty back together again. By itself it will not be sufficient: It will not hold over time; it will, however, buy time. But though a necessary step, it should not and cannot be the destination.

After all, Humpty was an egg.

INDEX

influence - which face of power?

Menu of choice for countries
re: economics